FILM reviews

"One of the most moving pieces I've seen all year."

– John Petrakis, *Chicago Tribune*

"If this well-done collection of four shorts was on paper instead of film, you'd find it in the pages of *The New Yorker or Atlantic Monthly*. Writer-director Greg Pak focuses on our contemporary computerized lives—occasionally delving into the future—in a weighty and relevant anthology."

– Laura Kelly, *Fort Lauderdale Sun Sentinel*

"*Robot Stories*' tagline is 'science fiction from the heart,' a phrase author and genre specialist Steven

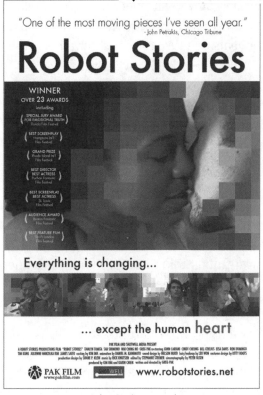

Robot Stories postcard

Schneider finds appropriate. '*Robot Stories* plays differently from a lot of the science-fiction films I've seen,' said Schneider … 'It made me reflect on science fiction's deep and long-standing romantic side. Greg is less interested in trying to pull the wool over our eyes by giving us something spectacular-looking than he is in exploring human relationships.'… In fact, 2004 may end up being American cinema's year of the robot, with Pak and his independent sci-fi movie getting the jump on Hollywood."

– Jason Silverman, *Wired.com*

"Forget *Hellboy*. *Robot Stories* is the real deal—a science-fiction with a brain and a heart."

– Ed Blank, *Pittsburgh Tribune-Review*

"If only Steven Spielberg had had the quirkiness and the funny bone of New York filmmaker Greg Pak when he set out to make *A.I.: Artificial Intelligence* a couple of years ago. We might all have been the richer for it."
– Michael Janusonis, *Providence Journal*

"In less than 90 minutes, *Robot Stories*... says more about humanity's relationship to machines than the entire *Matrix* trilogy. At its best, this quartet of vignettes could also be favorably compared to *Minority Report* (without the budget) and *A.I.* (without the bluster)."
– Joe Williams *St. Louis Post-Dispatch*

"Greg Pak's lovely, low-key science-fiction film has more in common with the short stories of Ray Bradbury than the pyrotechnics of George Lucas. Composed as a quartet of expertly acted chapters, the film's a smart evocation of love in the near-future, told through a widower's grief, a mother's anxiety, a family's tragedy, and a robot's confusion."
– Bilge Ebiri and Logan Hill, *New York Magazine*

"Ostensibly about artificial life forms, each of these four short, expertly crafted stories offers a poignant perspective on what it means to be human....Following in the footsteps of Ray Bradbury, Rod Serling and Philip K. Dick rather than George Lucas, Pak returns to the tradition of intelligent, humanistic sci-fi and reminds us of the value of good genre fiction."
– Ken Fox, *TV Guide*

"... these four segments cumulatively offer something much more satisfying than most sci-fi blockbusters. George Lucas could learn something from Pak and his predominantly Asian-American cast about creating credible characters..."
– Anthony Allison, *Las Vegas Mercury*

"Director Greg Pak's *Robot Stories* is the most entertainingly humanistic robot film since *Metropolis*, and anyone who tells you otherwise is probably a replicant and not to be trusted around small animals and electrical outlets."
– Marc Savlov, *Austin Chronicle*

"It will be interesting to see what Pak can do with a film that gets a little more funding and wider release. Then again, a big studio and a big budget wouldn't have improved *Robot Stories*. It's fairly close to perfect already."
– Peter Hartlaub, *San Francisco Chronicle*

"…smart, low budget meditation (or meditations) on love, loss, family, and community, writer director Greg Pak's anthology borrows elements from Ray Bradbury, Phillip K. Dick, and other sci-fi visionaries, but places them in a recognizable, down-to-earth context….*Robot Stories* isn't slick, isn't gimmicky. These are tales from the heart—pulsing to a high-tech beat."
– Steven Rea, *Philadelphia Inquirer*

"Built around the themes of love, death, family, and of course robots, Korean director Greg Pak's *Robot Stories* beautifully styles four tales. Through narratives both hilarious and touching, humans are forced to interact with robots in a way that eerily reflects the growing influence technology has on our lives….Each story is stunningly executed and moving in its own right."
– Melissa McCartney, *San Francisco Bay Guardian*

"Each of the stories, impeccably staged and acted, has just the right length….Never allowing preciousness or ponderousness to infuse the material, filmmaker Pak demonstrates a real talent for concise storytelling marked by poignancy and humor."
– Frank Scheck, *Hollywood Reporter*

"By turns funny, melancholy and incredibly moving."
– Katie Haegele, *Philadelphia Weekly*

"Strong thesping by a largely Asian American cast and clever sci-fi concepts…Helmer Greg Pak understands the short form well, mercifully avoiding blatant O. Henry twists while pulling off neat reversals of expertly set-up genre expectations."
– Ronnie Scheib, *Variety*

" 'The Robot Fixer' is truly transcendent….A poignant tale of love and loss."
– Pam Grady, *Contra Costa Times*

"… this is a heartfelt endeavor, given weight by [Sab] Shimono's extraordinary performance, in which the actor uses the subtlest flicks of his weary brow to call forth torrents of sorrow and minefields of regret."
– Scott Foundas, *LA Weekly*

"*Robot Stories* is composed of four separate, exemplary tales about the nebulous boundary between man and machine. An independent production devoid of expensive, and unnecessary, special effects, it offers crisp glimpses into a near future in which the intelligence is artificial but the emotion is real."
– Steven G. Kellman, *San Antonio Current*

"Director-writer Greg Pak's quartet of short films about the intersection of mechanized men with human nature is sensitively directed, beautifully acted and—unusual for most science-fiction movies—gracefully rendered."
– Gene Seymour, *Newsday*

"Pak loves the high concept, but keeps it simple; we're sucked in not by the conceit, the gimmick, but the emotion behind each tale, and it's a remarkable bit of work."
– Robert Wilonsky, *Dallas Observer*

"This is postmodern anthropology, a strange and bittersweet little movie that knows its sci-fi ancestry but dares to take it into new and personal directions. You'll want to follow along."
– Steve Schneider, *Orlando Weekly*

"*Robot Stories* explores people's humanity by setting it against a mechanical backdrop, without once resorting to cliche."
– Robb Bonnell, *Honolulu Weekly*

"Extremely great."
– Harry Knowles, *AintItCoolNews.com*

"One of the most human and humane science fiction films I've seen in a long time."
– Kathi Maio, *Magazine of Fantasy & Science Fiction*

"[The film's] four loosely interwoven stories about robots, parents, children and toxic workplaces contain enough intriguing notions about artificial intelligence and human relationships to fuel at least an hour's worth of happy post-movie geeking out."
– Wendy Banks *Now Toronto*

ROBOT STORIES
and more screenplays

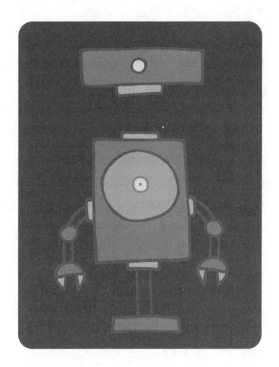

Greg Pak

Immedium
SanFrancisco

inspiring a world of imagination

Immedium, Inc.

P.O. Box 31846

San Francisco, CA 94131

www.immedium.com

First paperback edition published 2005.

Edited by Don Menn
Designed by Yon Sim

Manufactured in the United States of America
10 9 8 7 6 5 4 3 2 1

Library of Congress Control Number: 2004112738

ISBN: 1597020001

TABLE of contents

LIST of photos

FOREWORD

In 2000, I was rehearsing a Broadway musical when I received the phone call: "Hi, this is Greg Pak." I had met Greg when he shot an episode of *Asian America*, a PBS series for which I sometimes conduct interviews. He explained he was making a digital short, in which the lead character would be, well, me. "I could get someone to play David Henry Hwang," he continued, "but I thought you might want to do it yourself." Needless to say, this is not the kind of phone call one gets every day.

Greg pitched his concept for the short: an infomercial spoof in which I'd be the celebrity pitchman for "progressive pornography featuring smart Asian women and sexually empowered Asian men." Ever since the ethnic power movements of my college days, Asian men have complained of being stereotyped as emasculated and asexual by mainstream American culture. In one short film, it seemed Greg would be both illustrating and parodying these protests.

The result of Greg Pak's erudition in contemporary post-colonial theory is *Asian Pride Porn*, one of the screenplays in this volume. I did end up accepting his offer to play myself—who could resist? In a movie only a few minutes long, Greg succeeded in bringing together esoteric academia, political commentary, and populist SNL sketch humor into an imaginative and hilarious ménage.

A similar eclecticism characterizes all of Greg Pak's work, which continually juxtaposes unlikely themes and characters to discover surprising connections and new truths for our changing world. In case the name hasn't tipped you off, Greg is Asian American—Korean American, to be exact. Like the best artists of his generation, however, he does not feel compelled to agonize over the old issues of identity, assimilation, racism, or inter-generational conflict. His work takes as a given that Asians are part of the American fabric, that we have been changed by mainstream culture, and in turn transformed it as well. In Greg's films, those who earnestly fight dusty battles over political correctness often come in for the lion's share of satire: The Asian filmmaker in *Rice World* who uses his commercials for the Rice Association to promote racial harmony, the media watchdogs who protest his work as racist, or my character peddling *Asian Pride Porn*.

Yet Greg's very refusal to conform to established expectations for Asian American work makes his films deeply political. One can read the screenplay for his beautiful and haunting first feature-length film, *Robot Stories*, without noting the ethnicity of his characters. They are simply people (or simply robots) struggling to cope with a future where the distinction between humans and machines grows increasingly blurry. In the finished film, however, all the lead characters are Asian American. This juxtaposition raises a wealth of provocative questions: Can society view us as "simply people"? Can we see ourselves as central players and prime movers in an American setting? To what extent do the characters' ethnicities

Greg Pak in "Machine Love" segment of *Robot Stories*

enrich the film's more explicit plot elements? Is Archie (played in the movie by Greg himself) ridiculed, treated as a workhorse automaton, and desexualized by his (mostly white) co-workers because he's an android, or because he's an Asian male? Does he finally find humanity and sexual fulfillment with Lydia because she too is a robot, or because she too is Asian American? In each of his *Robot Stories* tales, Greg's use of Asian American characters generates a subversive subtext, forcing us to re-examine our roles in contemporary society.

All the screenplays in this volume challenge expectations in one provocative way or another. Even the most fanciful piece, the short *All Amateur Ecstasy*, teases us with one outcome, only to deliver a completely different climax to great comic effect. *Corporis Vesalius*, his study of a 16th-century Spanish pioneer of modern anatomy, presents biographical incidents out-of-sequence to elicit rich thematic and emotional connections. *Mouse* and *Catfight Tonight* examine romantic relationships through unlikely third-parties (in both cases, of the four-footed variety) which reflect back realities both couples seem unwilling to face directly. One definition of intelligence is the ability to wrap one's mind around contradictory notions; by this measure, Greg Pak's films exemplify contemporary wit and wisdom in our evolving world culture.

Film directors constantly ask themselves where to place the camera. Greg Pak's screenplays also ask us where we have placed our points of view. Taking new and surprising vantage points, Greg ends up engaging even classic Asian American themes—identity, assimilation, inter-generational conflict—in ways which look to the future rather than the past. The artificial beings in *Robot Stories*, for instance, surely presage confusions and joys already overtaking our technologically-obsessed culture. His pieces can prove prophetic in other ways as well: about the time Greg was conceiving *Asian Pride Porn*, a U.C. Davis Asian American studies professor, Darrell Hamamoto, wrote an essay, "The Joy F**k Club," which proposed combating the American media's emasculation of Asian males by producing "yellow porn." In 2003, Prof. Hamamoto realized his dream by actually shooting an all-Asian American skin flick. Does that make *Asian Pride Porn* a joke, a sociopolitical comment, or a vision of future reality? In the work of Greg Pak, the answer is almost always: all of the above.

David Henry Hwang
January 2005
New York City

David Henry Hwang is the Tony Award-winning playwright of "M. Butterfly," "Golden Child," "FOB," Disney's "Aida," and the Broadway revival of "Flower Drum Song."

PREFACE

During my second year of studying history at Oxford University, I wrote and directed a 50 minute superhero movie on BetaSP video called *Random Man*. The cast and crew were great and the production was a tremendous experience for a beginning film maker learning how to make an ambitious project come together with scant resources.

But the script was a mess.

I can still get a kick out of many aspects of the *Random Man* screenplay. Its central notion of a superhero with the power to generate completely random events in times of crisis still makes me chuckle. There's something weirdly compelling about the setting, a dystopian university town in which students tear up books rather than read them. And I can appreciate its effort to use a genre picture to tackle questions of politics and race. But the story features too many characters with ill-defined motivations, too many speeches, too much exposition, and too much cool stuff that doesn't quite add up. In short, it was a first draft. And I didn't know enough to be able to identify the script's problems or figure out how to address them.

At the time, I was capable of producing the occasional fine moment as a writer and director. Years of doing improvisational comedy as an undergrad at Yale and as a grad student at Oxford gave me confidence in building scenes, writing dialogue, and working with actors. And through decades of writing short stories, drawing cartoons, reading books, and watching movies, I'd developed some skill with narrative and visual storytelling. But I had a huge amount to learn.

Luckily, a few months after finishing *Random Man*, I entered the graduate film program at New York University where I was surrounded for the first time by film industry professionals who were prepared to tell me exactly what was wrong with my work and challenge me to reach the next level.

Eight years later, I finally entered production with my first feature film, *Robot Stories*, an anthology picture made up of four stories about love, death, family... and robots. *Robot Stories* has played in 75 film festivals, won 35 awards (including three screenwriting prizes), screened theatrically in limited release across the country, and is now available on DVD from Kino International.

The screenplays you're about to read were written between 1996 and 2001 and represent a good part of my journey from *Random Man* to *Robot Stories*. Each screenplay has its strengths—most were made into award-winning films or won prizes on their own. And of course, each screenplay has its flaws. I hope that reading them will help fellow writers, intrigue filmgoers interested in how a script turns into a movie, satisfy *Robot Stories* fans who want to delve more deeply into the film, and provide those involved with Asian American media with one director's ideas and strategies for tackling the question of Asian American representation on the big screen.

The screenplays have been arranged chronologically, but readers should free to read the book in any order which makes sense to them. In particular, anyone particularly averse to "spoilers" might prefer to read the each screenplay's introduction *after* reading the screenplay in question.

Many thanks to all my NYU professors for helping me start to learn the hard lessons. Many thanks to my classmates from NYU and fellow filmmakers from the Asian American Filmmakers Collaborative and the KMSG (a group of filmmakers known as the Korean Men's Support Group) for continuing to challenge me to get better. Many thanks to the Pollyannas, my producers Karin Chien and Kim Ima, and to all the cast and crew members who have worked on my projects over the years. And a tip of the hat to every film festival, curator, or distributor who has ever programmed my work and to every audience member who has taken the time to watch it.

Greg Pak
March 2005
New York City

EDITOR's note

For a film based upon a book, the eternal debate is whether the book was better than the film or vice versa. Though most films aren't based upon a book, every film is based upon a screenplay. And, even though annual awards are given for "Best Original" or "Adapted Screenplay," most moviegoers have never read a film script. If this is your first time, good for you!

Reading screenplays is an acquired taste, and quite a different experience than reading a book. It requires looking through the eyes of the director, cinematographer, and audience at the same time, and juggling the changing perspectives of actors, scenes, and sets. However, plain typewriter font, script jargon, and constantly interrupted narrative may not be very "user-friendly" to a modern audience used to the convenience of desktop publishing, online dictionaries, and hyperlinks.

Therefore to make this collection from Greg Pak more accessible, we have revised the traditional screenplay format. Cinematic purists may find these changes to be sacrilegious, but we hope they make your reading experience easier, and ultimately more rewarding.

We have updated the typical script presentation in a number of ways:
  A. The font is Frutiger, a modern style compatible with the collection's contemporary tone.
  B. Scenes and transitions are underlined in bold, so they are instantly recognizable.
  C. Character names are in bold when the characters have dialogue.
  D. On the following page Greg explains key screenplay terms and conventions.

So ultimately we hope that you enjoy reading Greg's work, and can then join into the eternal jawboning that so often begins, "The screenplay was better than the film…in its own way!"

A FEW WORDS on screenplay writing format

Screenplay writing comes with its own terms, conventions, and abbreviations which may need some explanation for new readers.

The SCENE HEADING is the capitalized series of words at the beginning of each new scene in a screenplay. Typically, it opens with INT or EXT, abbreviations for "interior" or "exterior," indicating whether things are happening indoors or outdoors, followed by a description of the location (for example, BEDROOM) and an approximation of the time (for example, DAY or NIGHT). Within a scene, subordinate headings may appear on their own lines and also in all caps to indicate different areas of the same location (for example, ACROSS THE ROOM or IN THE KITCHENETTE).

FADE IN and FADE OUT are transitional headings that indicate an emerging from or dissolving to black. Screenplays traditionally open with FADE IN. FADE TO BLACK is an often-seen variation, most commonly used at the very end of a script. DISSOLVE TO is another transitional heading, indicating a dissolve from one image or scene to another. CUT TO indicates a straight cut and is usually technically unnecessary, as every new scene heading implies CUT TO. JUMP CUT TO indicates a jarring hop from one moment in a shot to a moment in the same shot some time later.

PARENTHETICALS are brief notes or directions appearing in parentheses after a character's name and before the character's dialogue. Typically, PARENTHETICALS focus on emotional nuance and are used sparingly. I'll often use the term "beat" within PARENTHETICALS to indicate a small pause in the dialogue. Other parentheticals include (O.S.), for dialogue from characters who are off screen, (V.O.), for voice over, and (cont'd), used when a character's speech has been interrupted by action.

ANGLE ON and CLOSE ON indicate the camera angle the writer prefers for a given moment. ANGLE ON indicates that the camera cuts to whatever follows. CLOSE ON indicates a cut to a close-up of a character's face. Other variations include MEDIUM on for a medium shot (typically waist up) and WIDE ON for a wide shot (full body or wider).

These designations are generally used sparingly — typically, writers leave it up to directors to decide on camera angles for themselves. I rarely use the terms, even though I'm usually directing my own work, because too much explicit camera direction tends to bog down the reading experience. I find that I can get largely the same effect by simply starting a new paragraph when I imagine a cut to another image.

Screenplays have their own rules for CAPITALIZATION. Typically, the first time a character appears, his or her name or designation appears in all capital letters (for example, EXECUTIONER). In subsequent appearances, his or her name or designation has only the first letter capitalized (Executioner). All caps are also used for sound effects, for example, when a GUNSHOT hits the air. All caps can also be used (sparingly) any time something particularly important or surprising needs emphasis.

1. MOUSE
introduction

I made *Mouse* in 1997, during my third year of film school, at a time when I was editing *Fighting Grandpa*, a documentary about my Korean grandparents which I'd been working on since my second year. *Mouse* was a breakthrough project for me, the film through which I began to develop many of the principles which have guided my writing ever since.

One of the principles I'd internalized from years of doing improvisational comedy with groups like the Purple Crayon of Yale and the Pollyannas in New York City was that sometimes the best stories come from fully exploring a single crazy idea. In improv, scenes often fall apart when people pile on wacky elements rather than explore what's already out there. A scene in which someone discovers that his toaster can talk has plenty going on already. Adding a flying snake, the melting of the polar ice caps, and Albert Einstein might get some confused laughter, but it probably won't help the scene get to the potentially hilarious and emotionally resonant questions of what the toaster wants and what our hero's going to do about it.

At the time I was writing *Mouse*, I was struggling to make sense of the multiplicity of threads and voices in *Fighting Grandpa*. And I was very aware of having been trapped by the overly ambitious plot of *Random Man* years before. *Mouse* gave me the chance to apply my improviser's principle of more-through-less to a film project, to clear my brain by working on a very simple story. By paring things down, I could then apply another principle from improv—the notion that the best stories have both *text* and *subtext*.

The text (or plot-driven narrative) of *Mouse* came from the everyday experience of a rodent infestation in a New York apartment. I knew the situation could provide some fun, cinematic action. But the story only came together when the idea of pregnancy as subtext occurred to me. Our young hero Dan would be trying to catch a mouse—but what he'd *really* be trying to do was escape a conversation about pregnancy with his girlfriend Joyce. Suddenly the story had text and sub-

Seung-Hwan Han in *Mouse*

text; suddenly I could contrast what the characters *appeared* to be doing with what they were *really* doing. The gags became funnier because there was a real emotional story to follow, with higher stakes and multiple meanings and motivations. And resonant symbols naturally arose—our hero jabs at the mouse with a coat hanger because that's a natural reaction when a mouse runs under the stove, but with pregnancy as the subtext, the coat hanger and the unspoken notion of a "bun in the oven" took on a new symbolic power.

Mouse also let me explore the notion that bad behavior can make for great drama and the most compelling characters are often the most flawed people on the screen. The hero of *Mouse* is far from admirable, but his everyday cowardice is immediately recognizable, fun to watch, and dramatically compelling.

Finally, *Mouse* gave me the chance to grapple with Asian American representation in a new way. To this day, most Asian American characters in mainstream media fall into a few stereotypical categories: geisha girls and dragon ladies, gang lords and martial artists, nerds and technicians, deli owners and delivery boys. It's a boring set of stock depictions which reinforces notions of Asians as perpetually foreign, inscrutable, secondary bit players, ancillary to the American experience.

One way to fight these stereotypical representations is to call them out, to talk about them, to raise a ruckus. But while argument and activism can force *political* change, *personal* transformation remains elusive. Very few of us change our minds because of *intellectual* discussion or argument. Most of us only shift our beliefs when we've been hit by an undeniable *emotional* experience. So filmmakers actually have another, subtler way to reach people—by telling emotionally honest stories which involve three-dimensional characters. That's the tactic I tried in *Mouse*.

Mouse features two Asian American characters in a story that on the surface has nothing to do with so-called Asian American issues. On a deeper level, the film arguably has a specifically Asian American subtext, grappling with notions of Asian male silence and questions of communication between the sexes. But the tactic was to draw viewers in first and foremost by a universally compelling *visceral* story of a dude chasing a mouse and a universally compelling *emotional* story of a couple arguing about sex and responsibility. A wider audience with no prior interest in questions of Asian American representation might thus be pulled into identifying with the film's three-dimensional and non-stereotypically entertaining Asian American characters.

To date, *Mouse* has screened in 40 film festivals, won seven awards, including a Screenwriting Craft Award from NYU, been broadcast on television in the United States and Japan, and can be seen as an extra on the *Robot Stories* DVD.

But fellow screenwriters may note that despite its success, *Mouse*, like all my films, taught me a great deal through its shortcomings. Just one example: After seeing the finished film dozens of times at film festival screenings, I realized what was bothering me about the scene in which Dan reads aloud from a newspaper article about an abortionist. The scene introduces the theme of pregnancy and abortion, which is fine, but there's no character-based motivation for Dan to start reading the article aloud when he does. Generally, audiences accept the moment—mainly because the actors Seung-Hwan Han and Jo Shui play it so well. And the fact that Dan chucks the paper at the mouse in the next scene helps make the paper's introduction feel slightly less random. But the paper-reading scene remains inelegant, a contrived way of putting a theme into play. In retrospect, a better solution might have been to have had *Joyce* read the article—she knows her period is late and this would be her subtle way to try to gauge Dan's possible reaction.

MOUSE

FINAL DRAFT
1997

FADE IN.

INT. KITCHEN - NIGHT

DAN, a young man in a dingy New York apartment, kneels down in front of the stove, an untwisted and stretched-out coat hanger in his hand.

Dan peers through the vents at the base of the stove.

> **DAN**
>
> Little bastard.

Dan jabs the coat hanger through the vents. He thrashes the hanger around violently, then pauses.

> **WOMAN (O.S.)**
>
> Dan?

> **DAN**
>
> Hang on.

SILENCE as Dan peers into the darkness under the stove.

> **WOMAN (O.S.)**
>
> You get him?

Dan grunts with dissatisfaction and stands up.

> **DAN**
>
> I dunno. Can't hear a thing.

In the murky darkness under the stove, a small MOUSE blinks and twitches its whiskers.

INT. DAN'S BEDROOM - NIGHT

JOYCE, a young woman lying on the bed, looks up from her newspaper as Dan enters the room.

> **JOYCE**
>
> Maybe it was just a dust ball or something.

DAN

Dust balls don't run across the floor, Joyce.

He shudders.

DAN

Fucking mouse.

Joyce chuckles.

JOYCE

I wouldn't have thought you'd get so freaked out over a mouse.

DAN

(defensive)

Well, I'm not exactly jumping on chairs or anything.

JOYCE

Close enough.

DAN

No, I think I'm --

Joyce jerks up and points to the ground behind Dan.

JOYCE

Look out!

Dan spins.

DAN

Shit!

There's nothing in sight.

Joyce bursts into laughter.

DAN (cont'd)

(sarcastic)

Very funny.

> **JOYCE**
>
> Sissy boy.

> **DAN**
>
> Yeah, whatever.

She smiles and holds out a hand.

> **JOYCE**
>
> C'mere.

> **DAN**
>
> What.

> **JOYCE**
>
> C'mere.

Dan smiles, steps forward, and slips his arms around her waist.

> **DAN**
>
> So you like sissy boys, huh?

She giggles. They fall back onto the bed.

From the corner of the doorframe, a small MOUSE watches as Dan and Joyce embrace.

DISSOLVE TO:

INT. BEDROOM - LATER

Lying in bed, Dan picks up Joyce's paper. The headline reads:

"PRO-LIFERS PICKET DOCTOR'S HOME"

Dan frowns.

> **DAN**
>
> Jerks.

Joyce rolls toward him with a yawn.

JOYCE

What?

Dan reads from the paper.

DAN

"For the third week in a row, pro-life activists have marched outside the home of Donald Fung, a Flushing doctor who has performed over five hundred abortions in the past five years."

(beat)

I can't believe that shit.

JOYCE

Yeah, that's a lot of abortions isn't it?

Dan gives her a surprised look.

DAN

What?

JOYCE

What.

Dan taps the paper.

DAN

Don't tell me you think they're right.

Joyce gives Dan a mild smile.

JOYCE

Did I say that?

DAN

Well, you...

JOYCE

Just 'cause you're pro-choice doesn't mean you're pro-abortion.

Dan blinks.

DAN

Yeah, I know that.

JOYCE

I mean, if I got pregnant, I wouldn't get an abortion.

DAN

Really.

JOYCE

Yeah.

Dan blinks at her, a little thrown.

JOYCE (cont'd)

Does that bother you?

A tiny SHADOW darts across the doorway of the bedroom.

Dan jerks up.

DAN

Jesus!

JOYCE

What?

DAN

Goddamn mouse.

Dan grabs the paper and cautiously moves across the room.

JOYCE

Hey! Gimme back my paper!

DAN

Shhh!

INT. KITCHEN - NIGHT

Dan steps into the kitchen and flicks on the light.

There's no mouse in sight.

> **DAN**
>
> Damn.

> **JOYCE (O.S.)**
>
> You see him?

Dan bats the garbage can aside: no mouse.

> **DAN**
>
> No.

Dan scowls and whacks the garbage can with the newspaper.

> **JOYCE (O.S.)**
>
> Come back here.

Dan's eyes fall on the newspaper article.

> **DAN**
> (under his breath)
>
> Fuck.

> **JOYCE (O.S.)**
>
> Dan?

INT. COMMON ROOM - LATER

Dan pulls on his shoes. Joyce eyes him balefully.

> **JOYCE**
>
> Can't this wait until tomorrow?

> **DAN**
>
> Are you kidding?

JOYCE

We were in the middle of a conversation, Dan.

DAN

Look, Joyce, I'm not gonna let a dirty little mouse take over my apartment.

EXT. STREET - NIGHT

Dan, hunched up in his thin coat, stomps down the street.

EXT. DRUGSTORE - NIGHT

Dan steps out of a drugstore and pulls a few MOUSETRAPS out of a paper bag.

He smiles tightly to himself and shoves the traps back into his bag.

His eyes fall on the display in the window.

The sign reads:

SPECIAL: PREGNANCY TESTS $4.99

Dan's face falls.

He walks away.

INT. KITCHEN - NIGHT

Dan gingerly slides a cheese-baited mousetrap behind the garbage can, then looks up to see:

A tired, pajamaed Joyce leaning against the counter, idly eating cheese.

DAN

Joyce! Don't eat that.

Dan takes the cheese from her hands.

JOYCE

Hey!

Dan puts the cheese back in the refrigerator.

DAN

We gotta save this.

JOYCE

How much cheese can one mouse eat?

DAN

There're supposed to be ten hiding somewhere for every one you see.

JOYCE

I don't even think there's one.

DAN

What?

JOYCE

I haven't seen him.

Joyce opens the refrigerator and pulls out the cheese.

JOYCE (cont'd)

But it's real convenient for you to have a mouse to chase around right now. I think you made him up.

DAN

What are you talking about?

JOYCE

What would you do if I got pregnant?

DAN

Jesus, Joyce.

JOYCE

I'm serious. You'd freak out, wouldn't you?

Dan grabs at the cheese.

DAN

Would you quit eating that?

Joyce stares at him, slams the cheese down on the counter with a BANG, and storms out of the room.

INT. BEDROOM - NIGHT

The faint sound of GNAWING hits the air as Dan peers into the bedroom.

Joyce lies in bed, eating crackers as she reads her book.

> DAN
>
> Hey.

Joyce looks up balefully.

> DAN (cont'd)
>
> How you doing?

> JOYCE

(with casual hostility)

> Fine.

> DAN
>
> Don't be like that.

> JOYCE
>
> How do you want me to be?

> DAN
>
> I dunno.

> JOYCE
>
> Sure you do.

> DAN
>
> What are we talking about, here?

> JOYCE
>
> You want me to get an abortion.

DAN

Joyce, you're not even pregnant.

JOYCE

How do you know?

Dan stares at her.

DAN

You're pregnant?

Joyce smiles: Psych!

JOYCE

No.

Joyce chuckles.

JOYCE (cont'd)

You should see your face.

DAN

What.

She gives him a smile and holds out a hand.

JOYCE

C'mere, sissy boy.

DAN

Jesus.

He gives her a weak smile and lies down beside her.

JOYCE

I'm a few days late, though.

Dan stares at her.

DAN

What's that mean?

> JOYCE
>
> Nothing. I tend to be kind of erratic.

INT. KITCHEN - NIGHT

A tiny SHADOW falls over the cheese in the mousetrap.

INT. BEDROOM - NIGHT

Joyce and Dan kiss.

A sharp SNAP hits the air.

Dan jerks up.

> JOYCE
>
> What?

> DAN
>
> Got him.

Joyce tries to hold onto Dan as he pulls away from the bed.

> JOYCE
>
> Dan...

INT. KITCHEN - NIGHT

Dan and Joyce look down at the trap. The trap is sprung but empty.

> JOYCE
>
> I bet you just set it wrong.

> DAN
>
> What's that supposed to mean?

> JOYCE
>
> Went off by itself. Very conveniently.

Dan scowls.

DAN

Look, I'm not the one playing mind games around here.

Joyce turns back toward the bedroom.

JOYCE

Whatever.

INT. BEDROOM - NIGHT

Dan and Joyce lie in bed, backs to each other.

Joyce turns to gaze at Dan's back.

Dan stares into the darkness, listening intently.

Joyce slides up to Dan and runs a hand down his chest.

Dan stops her hand before it reaches his crotch.

DAN

Un-uh.

JOYCE

What.

DAN

Shhh...

JOYCE

What?

DAN

I'm trying to listen...

Dan gazes across the room into the darkness.

Joyce gazes at Dan's back as he listens to the night.

JOYCE

What's so awful about it, Dan? Don't you think we'd have a cute baby?

She lays a hand on his side.

> JOYCE

Dan?

Dan takes hold of her hand and pulls her arm around him.

> DAN

Sure.

Joyce smiles and presses her face against the back of his neck.

A guilty expression creasing his forehead, Dan listens as Joyce settles down.

He heaves a faint sigh and closes his eyes.

INT. BEDROOM - LATER

A faint CRUNCHING sound hits the air.

Dan's eyes flick open.

The CRUNCHING continues. It's a brittle GNAWING, coming from below the bed.

Very carefully, Dan eases his head toward the edge of the bed and peers down at the floor.

Its head poking out from beneath the bed, a little MOUSE gnaws at a cracker on the floor.

> DAN

Fuck!

Dan makes a wild grab at the Mouse.

The Mouse ducks out of sight under the bed.

The bed heaves up from the floor.

Dan turns with horror to see an enormous MOUSE'S TAIL writhing from beneath the opposite side of the bed.

Joyce, tossed by the bucking bed, screams at Dan with fear and anger.

> JOYCE

Leave him alone!

INT. KITCHEN - NIGHT

An awful, snarling grin on his face, Dan jabs the coat hanger into the vent under the stove.

INT. BEDROOM - NIGHT

Joyce SCREAMS with pain.

INT. BEDROOM - NIGHT

Dan jerks awake. He's been dreaming.

He turns to gaze at Joyce sleeping beside him.

> **DAN**
>
> Christ.

The sound of GNAWING hits the air.

Dan holds his breath, then eases to the edge of the bed.

The gnawing stops.

Dan peers over the edge of the bed.

A MOUSE-GNAWED CRACKER lies on the floor.

There's no mouse in sight.

> **DAN**
>
> Fucking mouse.

INT. KITCHEN - NIGHT

Dan opens the cabinet under the sink and pulls out a pair of heavy work gloves.

INT. BEDROOM - NIGHT

Dan, wearing the work gloves, looks at the cracker on the floor, eases back onto the bed, and turns off the light.

> **JOYCE**
>
> What's going on?

> **DAN**
>
> Nothing.

> **JOYCE**
>
> C'mere.

Joyce sleepily reaches for Dan.

He holds her away with his gloved hands.

DAN

Hold up, Joyce.

JOYCE

What the hell...

DAN

Shhh.

JOYCE

Gloves?

DAN

Shhh.

JOYCE

What the fuck is wrong with you?

DAN

Shhh!

The GNAWING starts.

JOYCE

Don't you shush me!

Dan lunges over the edge of the bed.

JOYCE

Dan!

A sharp SQUEAK hits the air.

DAN

Jesus.

Joyce switches on the light.

Dan stares in shock at his gloved fist.

A MOUSE'S TAIL writhes from between two of his fingers.

JOYCE

Oh my God.

Dan staggers to his feet and runs from the room.

INT. KITCHEN - NIGHT

Dan pulls a plastic grocery bag from beneath the kitchen sink, thrusts the mouse inside without looking, sets the bag on the floor, and pounds it hard with his fist.

DAN

Fuck!

With each of Dan's punches, the dark smear of blood inside the bag spreads.

JOYCE

Dan!

Dan, his face twisted with fear and rage, turns to see Joyce staring down at him with horrified disgust.

INT. BEDROOM - NIGHT

Dan, still flushed and jumpy, lies in bed, staring at the ceiling.

The sound of a FLUSHING TOILET hits the air and Joyce enters the room.

DAN

Hey.

Avoiding eye contact, Joyce reaches across the bed and picks up her book.

DAN

(carefully)

See, Joyce, I wasn't making it up. I --

JOYCE

I got my period.

DAN

You...

A look of cowardly relief runs over Dan's face. He smiles and reaches out for her hand.

> DAN

Hey.

Joyce jerks away.

> JOYCE

Don't touch me.

She turns and walks out of the room.

> DAN

Hey, Joyce...

Dan sits up to see Joyce in the other room, pulling on her shoes.

> DAN

Where you going?

> JOYCE

Shut up. You'll scare the mice away.

> DAN

Joyce, what are you talking about? We got him.

She stares at him, sad and angry.

> JOYCE

Ten hiding for every one you see, remember?

(with great, painful contempt)

Sissy boy.

Joyce turns and disappears from sight.

> DAN

Joyce!

Dan stumbles out of bed as the light in the common room goes out.

> DAN

Hold up!

Dan steps into the common room as the front door of the apartment SLAMS shut.

DAN

Joyce!

Dan puts his hand on the doorknob as the muffled sound of the front door of the building SLAMMING shut hits the air.

Dan hesitates, then slowly shifts his hand from the doorknob to the latch.

Dan locks the door.

A cowardly smile of relief spreads over his face.

The sound of GNAWING hits the air.

Dan's face falls as he turns to stare into the darkness of the kitchen.

INT. KITCHEN - NIGHT

The GNAWING grows louder as we slowly approach the stove, drawing nearer and nearer, finally slipping past the coat hanger into the dark vent.

A HUNDRED MICE, SQUEAKING, GNAWING, and CHATTERING, crawl over each other in the murky darkness.

FADE TO BLACK.

END.

2. CORPORIS VESALIUS
introduction

During my last year at NYU, I learned that the Sloan Foundation was sponsoring a competition for student-written screenplays. At the introductory meeting, representatives from the Sloan Foundation explained that they were looking for non-stereotypical depictions of scientists and more interesting explorations of the scientific method. I don't know if any of the students in the room had any training in science. But an NYU professor encouraged us to think of the competition as an introduction to professional writing for hire, a chance to learn how to research and write about new material on demand.

As I began looking for a subject, I found myself researching the beginnings of science and medicine, those early moments when a single person with a keen mind and a willingness to ask the right questions could take enormous leaps forward. And in my reading, I kept coming across Andreas Vesalius, the 16th century Belgian surgeon commonly known as the founder of modern anatomy.

Vesalius's story had great elements—macabre dealings with corpses, conflicts between reason and faith, and a mysterious death on a desert island. My chief challenges were to write a period piece and to figure out the emotional story of a man about whose personal life very little is known.

I dealt with the challenge of writing a period piece by not worrying about it too much. I borrowed a strategy from *Amadeus*—even though my characters would have been speaking foreign languages, I wrote their dialogue largely in American vernacular, avoiding obvious anachronisms but otherwise trying to maintain a familiar rhythm and vibe. Authority figures, however, I wrote more formally—a bit like the *Star Wars* strategy of giving villains English accents.

To deal with the challenge of having a protagonist about whose personal life little is known, I simply treated it as an advantage. The fact that there was no definitive account of Vesalius's emotional journey freed me to find a compelling story that fit the material. Ultimately, I realized I was telling the story of a man who challenged the prejudices of his age in the name of truth—but who lacked the courage to carry his challenge through to the end. The story fit beautifully with the key facts in Vesalius's life—and even allowed me to find a character-based way to make sense of and find redemption in his dramatic but otherwise baffling death as a shipwreck victim.

CORPORIS VESALIUS

Winner of a Sloan Foundation Screenwriting Award

FINAL DRAFT
February 26, 1998

FADE IN.

EXT. OPEN SEA - NIGHT

Lightning flashes and thunder BOOMS.

Dark waves toss around bits of broken wood and fixtures from a sixteenth-century sailing ship.

ANDREAS VESALIUS, a gaunt, fifty-year-old man, gasps for air, struggling to keep his head above the water.

> **VESALIUS**
>
> God, not yet...

A wave surges over his face.

DARKNESS fills the screen.

The ROAR of the ocean fades away.

> **YOUNG MAN 1 (V.O.)**
>
> I am Prometheus! Titan of Knowledge! Light Giver! Fire Bringer!

> **YOUNG MAN 2 (V.O.)**

(sardonic)

> Vulture dinner.

Unseen Young Men CHUCKLE and RUSTLE.

INT. DARKENED ROOM - NIGHT

The smiling, blindfolded face of the First Young Man fills the screen. It's VESALIUS, twenty-five years earlier, now a cocky young university student.

> **VESALIUS**
>
> Come to me, children, and read forbidden truths from these my lips!

MIGUEL SERVETUS, a sharp-eyed young Spaniard, rolls his eyes.

> **MIGUEL**
>
> You are such an ass.

> **VESALIUS**
>
> Come on, Miguel. Put up or shut up.

MIGUEL

All right, try this.

Miguel presses something into Vesalius's hands.

Vesalius frowns, feeling the object, then grins, holding up a small, round bone.

VESALIUS

Patella. Easiest bone in the human body.

A mixed chorus of GROANS and CHEERS hit the air, and we pull back to see Vesalius's surroundings for the first time.

He's sitting amongst the broken funerary sculpture and scattered, dried bones of a CHARNEL HOUSE.

The pack of rowdy Young Men around Vesalius break into a clamor, laughing and arguing, waving bits of human skeletons in each other's faces. All the men are dressed in the loose blouses and tight pants of Renaissance university students.

WOLFGANG, a stocky young German standing atop a tomb, waves a CLINKING bag of money in the air.

WOLFGANG

Come on, gentlemen! You stump him once and you walk away with the whole bag! Who's next?

Another Young Man hands Wolfgang a coin and pushes a bone into Vesalius's hands. Vesalius snorts.

VESALIUS

Scapula. Left.

YOUNG MAN 3

Damn.

WOLFGANG

Next!

The Young Men whoop and holler, some exchanging money in side bets, others scrambling for more obscure bones among the rubble.

YOUNG MAN 4

Here you go.

VESALIUS

Second cervical vertebra.

WOLFGANG

(to Young Man 4)

Thank you for playing.

YOUNG MAN 4

Go to hell.

Wolfgang laughs.

YOUNG MAN 5

Try this.

VESALIUS

Tibia, middle section, both ends broken off. Nice try, though.

YOUNG MAN 5

Yeah, well.

MIGUEL

Here.

VESALIUS

(grinning)

Back for more punishment, Miguel?

Vesalius takes a small bone from Miguel.

VESALIUS (cont'd)

All right, what do we have here...

A confused look slips over his face.

The Students quiet down, watching him.

VESALIUS (cont'd)

Huh.

The Students mutter amongst themselves with growing excitement.

MIGUEL

I got you, you bastard.

VESALIUS

Hold on...

Wolfgang fingers the bag of money a little nervously.

Full of concentration, Vesalius probes the strange bone with his long, careful fingers.

WOLFGANG

Andreas?

MIGUEL

(grinning to the others)

I finally got him!

WOLFGANG

Andreas...

MIGUEL

Come on, Wolfgang! Pay up!

A wry smile slowly spreads over Vesalius's face.

VESALIUS

You little cheat.

MIGUEL

Who are you calling a cheat?

VESALIUS

Only human bones allowed, Miguel. You can leave your canine septums at home.

Vesalius pulls his blindfold off and tosses the bone at Miguel.

Miguel stares at him, then snorts, laughs, and slaps Vesalius on the shoulder.

> **MIGUEL**
>
> All hail Prometheus.

The Students roar and cheer.

> **MIGUEL (cont'd)**

(shaking his head)

> Marvel at the fire he brings us.

EXT. GRAVEYARD - NIGHT

The Young Men burst out of the charnel house, bearing Vesalius on their shoulders, a human pelvis balanced on his head as a crown and a femur thrust into his hand as a scepter.

> **GUARD (O.S.)**
>
> Who goes there?

Pandemonium as the Students bolt in all directions.

Vesalius, dropped to the ground, looks up as Wolfgang and Miguel vanish into the darkness.

> **WOLFGANG**
>
> C'mon, Andreas!

A GUARD appears between Vesalius and the others.

Vesalius turns and bolts around a crypt to find:

A group of burly GUARDS in his way.

> **VESALIUS**
>
> Oops.

INT. UNIVERSITY HALL - DAY

Vesalius stands in formal dress before a group of stern, robed PROFESSORS.

Professor SYLVIUS stares at him grimly.

SYLVIUS

If the decision were mine alone, Andreas Vesalius, your expulsion from the university would be guaranteed. But kinder souls than I have pleaded leniency. And since your esteemed father, the Apotheker to the Emperor, has guaranteed your future good behavior, this tribunal will issue no formal punishment.

Vesalius meekly turns to face ANDREAS VESALIUS, SR., his thin, precise, and deeply embarrassed father.

EXT. STREET - DAY

Vesalius and Vesalius, Sr. walk down the street.

VESALIUS

It's not as bad as they made it sound, Father.

VESALIUS, SR.

(with distracted stiffness)

Of course not.

VESALIUS

It was actually kind of an educational thing.

VESALIUS, SR.

Yes, indeed.

VESALIUS

We were playing this game, identifying bones. I was blindfolded, but you know what? I got 'em every time. See, they would --

VESALIUS, SR.

Andreas.

Vesalius, Sr. pauses and wipes his forehead with a kerchief.

VESALIUS, SR. (cont'd)

I'm sorry. I can't...

(beat)

>   You know I was born a bastard...

Vesalius looks around, embarrassed.

>   **VESALIUS**
>
>   Father...

>   **VESALIUS, SR.**
>
>   ... and only two years ago managed to remove this stain from our line. After thirty years of faithful service. Papers of legitimacy. Worked for them my whole life.

>   **VESALIUS**
>
>   Yes, I know...

>   **VESALIUS, SR.**
>
>   Then why...

He takes a shuddering breath.

>   **VESALIUS, SR. (cont'd)**
>
>   Why shame our good name?

Vesalius lowers his eyes.

EXT. DISSECTION AUDITORIUM - DAY

It's a bright Spring day. A crowd of bored students sit in a outdoor amphitheater as Professor Sylvius reads aloud at a podium emblazoned with the University of Paris seal.

Sylvius drones on, reading from a dusty old book labeled Galen's Anatomy.

>   **SYLVIUS**
>
>   ... as the immortal Galen writes, we open the abdominal wall to see ...

On the stage below the podium, a ham-handed SURGEON sloppily saws open the chest of a naked human corpse.

Vesalius, sitting in the front row, scowls.

Miguel leans forward, frowning.

MIGUEL

He's ripping the whole thing up.

WOLFGANG

Shh.

MIGUEL

You can't find a thing if you just hack away like that.

Vesalius cringes as Sylvius glances their way.

MIGUEL (cont'd)

(still staring at the Surgeon)

This is a joke.

VESALIUS

Would you shut up?

MIGUEL

What?

Sylvius clears his throat, staring at the trio.

Vesalius and Wolfgang shrink in their collars.

Miguel turns to meet Sylvius's stare.

Sylvius snorts and goes back to reading.

The Surgeon casually rips out a fistful of mangled innards.

Miguel gives Vesalius a contemptuous look.

INT. INN - DAY

Vesalius and Miguel sit at a table, drinking beer.

MIGUEL

So what are you telling me, you're happy to let incompetent old men waste your time?

VESALIUS

I didn't say that.

MIGUEL

You don't have to.

Wolfgang marches up to the table with a roast chicken on a platter.

WOLFGANG

Dinner is served.

Wolfgang sits down and tucks a kerchief into his collar. Noticing the silence, he follows Miguel's baleful stare to Vesalius's downcast face.

WOLFGANG (cont'd)

What's up?

Vesalius picks up the carving knife and carefully begins to separate out the bird's muscles.

WOLFGANG (cont'd)

Aw, come on, Andreas. I'm hungry.

MIGUEL

(staring at Vesalius)

The most talented student in Paris, and the biggest coward.

Vesalius jaw tightens, but he continues dissecting the bird.

MIGUEL (cont'd)

Some Light Giver.

Beat.

WOLFGANG

How 'bout we eat?

VESALIUS

Zeus punished Prometheus by strapping him to a rock and sending vultures to devour his liver.

MIGUEL

So.

VESALIUS

That probably hurt.

MIGUEL

The truth was worth it.

Vesalius continues probing the bird.

WOLFGANG

Okay. I'm gonna get another chicken.

VESALIUS

No.

A decisive look slips over Vesalius's features.

VESALIUS (cont'd)

We need a human body.

WOLFGANG

What?

Vesalius drops the knife, gets up from the table, and heads toward the door.

WOLFGANG (cont'd)

(to Miguel)

Did he say --

MIGUEL

(grinning)

Come on.

EXT. TOWN SQUARE - DAY

Vesalius and the others push their way through the crowd toward an executioner's gibbet set up in the center of the square.

WOLFGANG

Aw, no...

As the trio squeeze to the front of the crowd, a hooded EXECUTIONER approaches a trembling PRISONER.

The Executioner's blade flashes and the crowd SCREAMS.

EXT. STREET - NIGHT

Vesalius opens a door, peers out at the empty street, then motions with his hand.

Miguel and Wolfgang step out onto the street, toting a long, heavy bundle wrapped in heavy cloth.

> **WOLFGANG**
>
> This is so stupid.

> **MIGUEL**
>
> Shut up.

Vesalius, a head-sized bundle tucked under his arm, presses a bag of coins into the hand of the smiling Executioner and follows his friends down the street.

INT. BEDROOM - NIGHT

Wolfgang and Miguel sit on the floor, watching as Vesalius carefully cuts into the corpse of the Prisoner.

Vesalius grins as he gently and cleanly separates the abdominal muscles to expose the organs within.

> **VESALIUS**
>
> Now that's a little nicer, huh?

EXT. DISSECTION AUDITORIUM - DAY

Sylvius reads out loud from the podium.

Miguel and Wolfgang watch from the front row as:

Vesalius, on the stage in the Surgeon's place, expertly lifts out an organ from the innards of the corpse to display to the students.

> **MIGUEL**
>
> (smiling at Wolfgang)
>
> All hail Prometheus.

DISSOLVE TO:

EXT. LARGER DISSECTION AUDITORIUM - DAY

A University of Padua seal decorates the arch above the entrance of the auditorium.

Down on the stage, a slightly older, bearded Vesalius, now wearing a professor's robes, performs an intricate maneuver in his dissection, delicately separating out a network of veins.

A MURMUR of appreciation rises from the crowd.

Vesalius, Sr. beams at his son from the stands.

> **MIGUEL (V.O.)**
>
> He braves God's wrath to bring us fire.

As Vesalius looks up from the stage, his brow furrows.

A smiling MIGUEL stands at the top of the stands, rimmed with sunlight.

With a sharp CRACK, Miguel bursts into FLAME.

INT. BEDROOM - NIGHT

The fifty-year-old Vesalius jerks awake, panting and sweating.

The CRACK sounds again -- it's a KNOCK on the door.

> **VESALIUS**
>
> Damn it.

INT. HALLWAY - NIGHT

The fifty-year-old Vesalius buttons his shirt, marching down the hallway alongside an agitated PAGE.

> **PAGE**
>
> I'm sorry, sir, but you said if things got worse...

> **VESALIUS**
>
> Yes, yes...

A thin WAIL echoes down the hall. Vesalius and the Page exchange looks and break into a jog.

INT. SICKROOM - NIGHT

Vesalius bursts into the room.

The INFANTE, a seventeen-year-old Spanish prince, writhes prone in his sickbed, held down by his Spanish doctors, OLIVARES, VEGA, and DAZA CHACON.

A swollen, open WOUND festers on the back of the Infante's head.

PINTERETE, a tall, ornately dressed Moor standing on the other side of the bed, dips a brush into a bubbling pot of dark liquid.

> **VESALIUS**
>
> What in God's name is going on here?

> **PINTERETE**
>
> The holiest of healings.

> **VESALIUS**
>
> What?

> **DAZA CHACON**
>
> Your presence was not requested, Doctor Vesalius.

> **VESALIUS**
>
> Let the boy go!

> **OLIVARES**

(to Pinterete)

> You may proceed, Doctor.

Vesalius turns to the DUKE OF ALVA, a tall, brooding nobleman standing in the corner.

> **VESALIUS**
>
> Duke, please!

The Duke says nothing, staring grimly as Pinterete approaches the Infante.

The Infante twists to see Pinterete standing over him, brush in hand.

INFANTE

No!

VESALIUS

Stop this!

Pinterete daubs the Infante's wound with his brush.

The Infante lets out a piercing SCREAM.

VESALIUS (cont'd)

Dear God.

The Duke's jaw twitches. His whole body jerks as he slams his staff on the floor.

DUKE

Enough!

INT. DRAWING ROOM - NIGHT

Vesalius watches wearily as a group of GUARDS roughly usher Pinterete down the hall.

DAZA CHACON (O.S.)

Milord, successful treatments are often painful.

Vesalius turns to look into the drawing room. The Duke sits in the center of the room, surrounded by the Spanish Doctors.

DUKE

This is not healing.

DAZA CHACON

Milord...

DUKE

(sharply)

Even I could see the prince's skin blister and burn.

The Spanish Doctors fall silent.

VESALIUS

Your Grace.

The Duke regards him silently.

VESALIUS (cont'd)

Again, I beg your permission to make an attempt.

DAZA CHACON

Impossible.

VESALIUS

(eyes locked on the Duke)

Duke, please.

DAZA CHACON

Your Grace, this man stinks of death. His entire life has been devoted to abomination.

VESALIUS

Do we have to go through this again? Six years ago the faculty of Salamanca decreed in my favor. We all know that dissection is no sin.

DAZA CHACON

And now you presume to lecture us on theology! Duke, is this man's presence here not intolerable?

The Duke stands and walks to the window.

In the street below, a group of TOWNSPEOPLE stand vigil, holding candles and lanterns.

DUKE

He was the Emperor's physician.

DAZA CHACON

And you may remember how little his ministrations improved the Emperor's gout.

VESALIUS

(with growing anger)

> Correct me if I'm wrong, friends, but discussing my previous occupations and the late Emperor's afflictions will do very little to improve the health of the boy dying in the other room.

The Duke looks at Vesalius, a slightly shocked look on his face.

VESALIUS (cont'd)

(softening)

> Your Grace, please. You must allow me to examine the bone.

DAZA CHACON

> The Infante is not yet a corpse ready for your hacksaws.

VESALIUS

> With you in charge, he soon will be.

DAZA CHACON

> Good Doctor!

VESALIUS

> Duke, maybe the boy can still be saved. Give me your leave, I'm begging you.

The Duke gazes out the window. A new group of lantern-bearing Townspeople are approaching. On their shoulders they carry a long, narrow box: a coffin.

DUKE

> When the King left this palace to pray at San Jeronimo, I knew he believed only a miracle could save his son.

The Duke turns to the doctors.

DUKE (cont'd)

> Perhaps a miracle has come.

A confused look slips over Vesalius's face.

INT. MAIN HALL - NIGHT

The doors of the palace burst open and Townspeople crowd into the hall, carrying an open coffin containing an ancient, withered CORPSE wrapped in a tattered friar's robe.

> **TOWNSPERSON 1**
>
> San Diego will save the child!
>
> **VESALIUS**
>
> Dear God.

INT. SICKROOM - NIGHT

The Infante turns to stare with paralyzed horror as the Spanish doctors and various PRIESTS and Townspeople lower the corpse of San Diego into the bed beside him.

> **INFANTE**
>
> No, God, no!
>
> **PRIEST**
>
> Kiss the hand of San Diego, my prince! Kiss his hand and be healed!

The Infante tries to twist away from the corpse's bony arm.

> **INFANTE**
>
> No!

Vesalius turns away.

INT. BEDROOM - NIGHT

The Younger Vesalius, wrapped in a blanket on the floor, jerks awake as his head knocks against a:

FLAYED HAND, dangling from the bed.

Vesalius sits up, then chuckles, moves to the fire, lights a lantern, and walks back over to the bed.

A half-dissected CORPSE lies in the bed.

Vesalius scratches his belly, staring at the corpse, then hangs the lantern on a peg, pulls up a chair, and begins to work on the corpse's head, picking out inner structures with his scalpel, then meticulously drawing them on sheets of paper on his side table.

INT./EXT. BEDROOM - LATER

The sun rises over the town outside Vesalius's window.

At his bedside, Vesalius wipes his hands on a towel and leans over the side table to finish a diagram.

He gazes at his drawing, gazes at the corpse, then flips through a reference book: his worn tome of Galen's Anatomy.

> **VESALIUS**
>
> How about that...

EXT. UNIVERSITY SQUARE - DAY

Vesalius strides though the square, dogged by STUDENTS.

> **STUDENT 1**
>
> Professor, I hear they interred the burgomeister's mistress last night.

Vesalius's eyes light up.

> **VESALIUS**
>
> Really.

> **STUDENT 1**
>
> Yes, sir. Should I...

> **VESALIUS**
>
> Well, of course. But let's be careful, now.

> **STUDENT 1**
>
> (grinning)
>
> Yes sir.

Vesalius catches sight of a familiar figure stepping out of a university building

> **VESALIUS**
>
> Miguel! Miguel Servetus!

> **MIGUEL**
>
> Andreas Vesalius!

VESALIUS

What are you doing in Padua?

MIGUEL

Just passing through. I just got run out of Paris.

VESALIUS

What?

MIGUEL

They didn't like my views on astrology.

VESALIUS
(shaking his head)

You always have to pick the most shocking subject around, don't you?

MIGUEL

And you don't?

VESALIUS

I don't go looking for controversy.

MIGUEL

It just finds you.

Vesalius gives Miguel a look.

VESALIUS

Well. Maybe it did today.

INT. DISSECTION ROOM - DAY

Vesalius stands at a table, working on the severed head of a cow.

Miguel smiles as Vesalius's Students crowd around, elbowing each other for room to see.

VESALIUS

Now here's Galen's rete mirable, the eye muscle about which we've all heard so much.

Vesalius holds up the sketch he made in the morning.

VESALIUS (cont'd)

But here's what I found when I went looking for it in the human body.

The Students murmur among themselves. The structure in the cow's head and their professor's drawing are clearly different.

STUDENT 2

What, so Galen's wrong?

VESALIUS

Well, let's not say <u>wrong</u>.

(carefully)

The, ah, immortal Galen himself writes that his efforts were limited to dissecting animals. No doubt he found the structure in cows, perhaps apes, and assumed it was present in humans as well.

STUDENT 2

But it's not.

VESALIUS

Since we're fortunate enough to live in more enlightened times, we can consider the human body directly, and see how it differs from the lesser animals.

MIGUEL

(wryly)

So... Galen's wrong.

VESALIUS

Well...

The door bursts open, and the FIRST STUDENT runs inside, a corpse-sized bundle draped over his shoulder.

STUDENT 1

Got her!

The Students whoop as the First Student flops the body onto a dissection table.

VESALIUS

(to the First Student)

You could have waited until nightfall.

STUDENT 1

Aw, no one saw me. Besides, I don't think you'd want her if it took much longer.

The Students recoil, covering their noses as they peel the wrappings off of the corpse.

STUDENT 2

Sweet Jesus.

VESALIUS

No blasphemy, please. Now, would someone be kind enough to get me a clean knife?

INT. DISSECTION ROOM - LATER

Vesalius and his Students, kerchiefs tied over their noses and mouths, lean over the head of the corpse.

VESALIUS

We'll let the human body speak for itself, then.

(beat)

Everybody ready?

MIGUEL

If you are.

Vesalius eyes Miguel, then lets out a little snort and raises his scalpel to the corpse's face. As Vesalius begins to cut, the corpse's eyes fly open and a piercing SCREAM hits the air.

INT. SICKROOM - NIGHT

The Infante HOWLS, Vesalius's knife jutting from his head.

INT. BEDROOM - NIGHT

The fifty-year-old Vesalius's eyes fly open.

He's been dreaming.

INT. HALLWAY - NIGHT

A haunted Vesalius walks down the hallway toward the Infante's sickroom.

INT. SICKROOM - NIGHT

Vesalius steps into the darkened room.

The Infante lies on the bed, pale and sweating beside the withered corpse of San Diego.

Vesalius sits down beside the Infante. He gently moves the sheets to inspect the boy's wound, which is more livid than ever.

The Infante GROANS and rolls in his sleep.

The skin around the boy's eyes is discolored and grossly swollen.

> **VESALIUS**
>
> Good God.

> **VOICE (O.S.)**
>
> Doctor.

Vesalius turns to see the PHILIP, KING OF SPAIN, miserable and haggard in his royal robes, sitting in the corner of the room.

> **VESALIUS**
>
> King Philip...

> **PHILIP**
>
> Can you help him?

INT. SICKROOM - MORNING

Vesalius opens a small box and pulls out a thin scalpel.

His fingers tremble slightly.

> DAZA CHACON
> (under his breath)
>> How many corpses has that blade cut?

> DUKE
>> Silence.

The Spanish Doctors scowl.

Vesalius wedges a small bowl under the side of the Infante's cheek and raises the scalpel to the swollen tissue.

> DUKE (cont'd)
>> His Majesty the King has complete faith in Doctor Vesalius.

Vesalius gives the Duke a weak smile.

INT. DRAWING ROOM - DAY

King Philip buries his face in his hands as the Infante's thin WAIL echoes down the halls.

INT. PRINTING PRESS - DAY

The WAILING CREAK of the printing machine fills the air as the PRINTER works the lever back and forth.

A thirty-year-old Vesalius gazes with nervous excitement as the Printer carefully peels the first piece of paper from the plate.

Vesalius smiles as the picture comes into view.

It's a perfectly printed, intricately detailed woodcut of a skinless man standing in a life-like pose, all his muscles labeled with small letters.

> PRINTER
>> Beautiful, no?

> VESALIUS
>> Yes.

A MONTAGE:

PRINTERS set new plates into the machine and turn the lever.

From the innards of the machine, Printers peel away completed pages filled with dense writing and intricate drawings of skeletons, bones, muscles, and organs.

BINDERS arrange the pages into order and begin to stitch.

A Printer sets a beautiful, bound copy of the completed book down on the table with a satisfying WHUMP. The cover reads:

> *Andreas Vesalius*
>
> *De Humani Corporis Fabrica*

INT. LECTURE ROOM - DAY

Wolfgang, now a bearded professor, grins as he opens a copy of *The Fabrica* before a crowd of awed students.

INT./EXT. BOOKSTORE - DAY

Miguel smiles, gazing through the window at a group of learned MEN arguing excitedly over an open copy of *The Fabrica*.

INT. DRAWING ROOM - DAY

Sylvius, Vesalius's old professor, frowns as he pages through a copy of The Fabrica. As each beautifully detailed page flips by, his frown deepens.

EXT. DISSECTING ARENA - DAY

Vesalius steps out onto the stage of a hastily constructed dissecting arena. The packed crowd of STUDENTS behind the front row DIGNITARIES cheer.

Vesalius smiles and waves. The Students whoop and stomp their feet.

With a great CRACK, the overcrowded stands begin to collapse.

The Students, laughing and shouting, scramble to safety over the heads of the Dignitaries.

Vesalius laughs. He's on top of the world.

INT. IMPERIAL PALACE - DAY

Silent GUARDS stand watch in a long, ornate hallway filled with elaborate paintings and sculptures.

As we move down the hallway, Vesalius's VOICE becomes audible.

VESALIUS (O.S.)

And so the doctors, who now fancied themselves "physicians," chose just one branch of medicine, proscribing drugs and diets from their books. The rest of curing they left to the surgeons, whom they treated like menials.

INT. RECEIVING ROOM - DAY

The thirty-year-old Vesalius, a little nervous in his formal clothing, stands in the middle of the room, reading from the preface of *The Fabrica*.

His August Majesty, EMPEROR CHARLES V, sits on his throne, flanked by COURTIERS, SERVANTS, and GUARDS.

Vesalius, Sr., sits off to the side, nearly bursting with pride as he watches his son address the Emperor.

VESALIUS

Soon, these physicians became too comfortable to think of observing nature with their own eyes or dissecting a human body with their own hands.

Professor Sylvius, sitting a few chairs away from the Emperor, fixes Vesalius with a cold stare.

VESALIUS (cont'd)

Instead, they taught anatomy by reading Galen aloud from some high podium while an unschooled barber hacked at the corpse below.

Sylvius whispers into the ear of the Courtier at his side.

VESALIUS (cont'd)

But now that the gods have chosen you, Most August Caesar Charles, as the lord of this new age of great happiness...

As Vesalius watches, the Courtier whispers into Charles ear.

VESALIUS (cont'd)

...philosophy thrives again, and medicine reclaims her true glory --

CHARLES V
(interrupting)

> So that now we are blessed to have your remarkable book before us.
> Thank you, Doctor Vesalius, for your gracious words of dedication.

Vesalius opens his mouth to stammer his thanks, but Charles is already rising from his throne.

CHARLES V (cont'd)

> And now I believe the luncheon hour is upon us, is it not?

INT. BANQUET HALL - DAY

Vesalius sits beside Wolfgang and watches as Charles gorges himself on seafood and beer.

WOLFGANG

> I tell him time and time again that he can't handle cold beer and
> seafood.

Charles drains his flagon and slams it down on the table.

CHARLES V

> More!

Wolfgang chuckles.

WOLFGANG

> But Emperors will be Emperors.

Vesalius squirms, miserable and anxious.

VESALIUS

> I'm finished.

WOLFGANG

> Relax, Andreas.

VESALIUS

> They've turned him against me. They'll burn the book. They'll kick me
> out of the university.

WOLFGANG

Andreas. He just got hungry.

Vesalius, Sr. slips up to the table.

VESALIUS

(to his father)

What's going on?

VESALIUS SR.

(miserable)

You've been accused. Impiety, arrogance, falsehood.

VESALIUS

What?

VESALIUS SR.

"Venanus."

VESALIUS

What?

VESALIUS SR.

Instead of "Vesalius." They're saying "Venanus."

WOLFGANG

"Venanus"?

VESALIUS

Madman.

VESALIUS SR.

(blankly)

Madman. Idiot. Ass.

(beat)

Bastard.

Vesalius stares at his father, then lowers his eyes.

> **VESALIUS**
>
> I'm sorry, Father.

> **VESALIUS SR.**
>
> Sorry? No. Nothing to be ashamed of.

(beat)

> The book. Beautiful, really. I'm... I was amazed.

Vesalius smiles. His father smiles back.

> **VESALIUS SR. (cont'd)**
>
> Now then. It's all been arranged. In the Emperor's service. You'll be safe.

> **VESALIUS**
>
> In the what?

EXT. BATTLEFIELD HOSPITAL - DAY

Cannons BOOM and SOLDIERS SHOUT and SCREAM.

Under a makeshift tent, the thirty-year-old Vesalius holds a wounded Soldier down as Wolfgang raises a flaming torch to cauterize the man's wound.

The Soldier SCREAMS as the torch sears his flesh.

Wolfgang flashes a grin at Vesalius's horrified face.

> **WOLFGANG**
>
> Little louder than your usual patients, huh?

EXT. JOUSTING FIELD - DAY

A little older, Vesalius and Wolfgang sit at the bedside of a feverish NOBLEMAN.

> **WOLFGANG**
>
> What do you think?

> **VESALIUS**
>
> I don't know.

He gnaws on his lip, thinking.

VESALIUS (cont'd)

One more cup?

Wolfgang nods and positions a bowl beneath the Nobleman's arm.

Vesalius, his face creased with doubt and worry, lifts a knife and begins to bleed the man.

INT. DEATHBED - NIGHT

Now in his mid-thirties, Vesalius stands at an ailing BARON's bedside as a BARONESS howls with rage and grief.

BARONESS

What do you mean "hopeless"? Save him, damn you!

INT. SICKROOM - DAY

Still older, Vesalius swallows hard, then reaches down and gently closes the eyes of his dead father.

DISSOLVE TO:

INT. EMPEROR'S BEDROOM - DAY

A weary, forty-year-old Vesalius walks from the fitfully sleeping Emperor toward Wolfgang, who stands in the doorway.

They converse in whispers.

WOLFGANG

How is he?

VESALIUS

Dying.

WOLFGANG

Hmmm.

VESALIUS

I'm in hell.

WOLFGANG

You're doing better with him than any other doctor has.

Vesalius gazes across the room at the sickbed.

VESALIUS

I'm just a better guesser.

(beat)

We don't know anything, do we?

Wolfgang shrugs.

VESALIUS (cont'd)

I'm going to go back to the university.

WOLFGANG

Dig up some new truths?

VESALIUS

If I can.

WOLFGANG

Like Servetus.

VESALIUS

(smiling)

Miguel.

(beat)

You read his last book?

WOLFGANG

No. It was banned, as I recall.

VESALIUS

Well, yes, he goes a little overboard with the astrology and theology.
But there was part that was really interesting.

Vesalius smiles, warming to the subject.

VESALIUS (cont'd)

Funny idea. He argues that blood gets from one ventricle of the heart to the other through the lungs.

WOLFGANG

Andreas...

VESALIUS

The thing is that he could be right. I mean, I was never able to find any pores in the membrane between the ventricles. That little cheat could really be onto something.

(beat)

That's the kind of work I should be doing.

Wolfgang sighs.

WOLFGANG

If you want to get burned.

VESALIUS

What?

WOLFGANG

I just heard. Miguel. In Geneva. They sentenced him for heresy and burned him at the stake.

A GROAN comes from the other room.

A COURTIER steps forward.

COURTIER

Doctor...

Vesalius stands stunned.

Wolfgang stares into Vesalius's eyes.

WOLFGANG

Be smart, Andreas.

> **COURTIER**
>
> Please, Doctor...

Vesalius slowly turns and walks back toward the bed.

With each slow-motion step, Vesalius grows older, his beard graying, his hairline receding, his face thinning...

... and with each step, the covered bodies of DEAD PATIENTS drift past Vesalius, followed by groups of mourning NOBLES and COURTIERS.

His eyes becoming more and more sunken and haunted, Vesalius stares as the bodies and the years drift by.

DISSOLVE TO:

INT. SICKROOM - DAY

The fifty-year-old Vesalius, pale and drawn, sits at the bedside of the Infante.

King Philip steps into the room.

> **VESALIUS**
>
> Your Highness.

Slowly, Philip kneels down before the still body of the Infante.

He strokes the boy's bangs back, then smiles softly. The Infante sleeps gently, his eyes back to their normal size.

> **PHILIP**
>
> Thank God.

He looks up at Vesalius.

> **PHILIP (cont'd)**
>
> Thank you.

> **VESALIUS**
>
> No. Thank God.

Philip gives him a questioning look.

> **VESALIUS (cont'd)**
>
> He hit the back of his head. But his orbits filled with pus. Why? I don't know. I drained the pus and he got better. Why? I don't know.

> PHILIP

But you saved him.

Vesalius turns. His gaze falls on the flames flickering in the fireplace.

Deep sorrow and shame fill Vesalius's eyes.

> PHILIP (cont'd)

Doctor?

Vesalius presses his face in his hands.

> PHILIP (cont'd)

(softly)

How can I repay you?

Beat.

Vesalius slowly looks up.

INT. PALACE CHAMBER - DAY

King Philip sits at his throne, his son the Infante at his right and the Duke of Alva at his left. The Spanish Doctors sneer faintly as Vesalius, nervous and excited, kneels before the King.

> PHILIP

Doctor Vesalius, We thank you most deeply for your hand in restoring Our son to a state of health. And We accept with heavy heart but great good wishes your departure for Padua.

EXT. SHIP - DAY

Vesalius, his face full of eager anticipation, stands at the bow as the ship sails out over the sea.

> CHARLES V (V.O.)

We lose you as Our physician, but all the world will gain when you resume your work as Professor of Anatomy. God speed you and protect you.

EXT. OPEN SEA - EVENING

Skies darken. Lightning flashes. Thunder CRASHES.

Vesalius, gasping for air, slips under the surface of the water.

EXT. BEACH - MORNING

Vesalius, soaked through, walks quickly along the beach beside a concerned-looking OLD MAN.

> **OLD MAN**
>
> Almost there.

> **VESALIUS**

(distracted)

> I should be getting on to Padua.

> **OLD MAN**
>
> Just around the bend...

> **VESALIUS**
>
> I really...

A half-naked, emaciated MAN comes into view, lying under a scraggly tree. Vesalius's brow furrows.

> **OLD MAN**
>
> Can you save him?

> **VESALIUS**
>
> I don't know.

Vesalius kneels down beside the Man.

> **VESALIUS (cont'd)**
>
> How are you feeling, friend?

The Man says nothing. But his hands roam over his thin frame, carefully feeling out his bones, so prominent beneath his skin.

Vesalius stares, confused.

The Man's fingers trace his naked chest.

Vesalius inhales sharply and closes his eyes.

DARKNESS.

> **VESALIUS (V.O.) (cont'd)**
>
> Sternum, of course.

INT. CHARNAL HOUSE - NIGHT

The young, blindfolded Vesalius laughs as Miguel, Wolfgang, and the other Students hand him bones.

> **VESALIUS**
>
> Left occipital. Right occipital. Sacrum, an unusual six-piece specimen, if I'm not mistaken.

EXT. BEACH - DAY

The emaciated Man lies on the beach, still tracing the bones of his own body.

The Man is the fifty-year-old Vesalius, all alone, on the verge of death.

> **VESALIUS (V.O.)**
>
> Radius. Ulna. Humerus. Clavicle. I know them all.

He opens his eyes and gazes into the sky.

> **VESALIUS (V.O.) (cont'd)**
>
> What else do you have for me?

A few VULTURES begin to spiral overhead.

Vesalius smiles.

> **VESALIUS (cont'd)**
>
> Of course.

Vesalius slowly parts his hands to expose his pale belly.

The waves gently crash onto the beach as the Vultures softly descend.

VESALIUS (V.O.) (cont'd)

Show me all of it, now...

Vesalius takes a breath, eyes open, a little nervous, but ready.

The Vultures flap to the ground beside him.

VESALIUS (V.O.) (cont'd)

I want to know everything.

TITLE CARD:

Shipwrecked on the Island of Zante,

Andreas Vesalius died in October 1564.

His masterwork, The Fabrica of the Human Body, marks the birth of modern observational science and research.

FADE TO BLACK.

END.

3. ASIAN PRIDE PORN
and other digital shorts introduction

I graduated from film school in 1998 determined to keep working as a filmmaker, no matter what. While I didn't have the money or resources to shoot anything as ambitious as *Corporis Vesalius* or any of the feature scripts I'd written, I was able to make two super-short 16mm films with my improvisational comedy group, the Pollyannas. But that broke the bank, and without grants or investors, it was unclear how or when I'd be able to make another film. Fortunately, my graduation coincided with the release of Apple's Final Cut Pro, the first reliable and affordable software for editing video on a home computer. With access to a MiniDV camera, a G3 Macintosh, and Final Cut Pro, I could suddenly make broadcast quality short films for a few hundred dollars apiece. So from 1999 to 2001, I made a series of short digital comedies, including *Asian Pride Porn*, *All Amateur Ecstasy*, and *Cat Fight Tonight*.

Asian Pride Porn was my contribution to an anthology of films called *Avenue of the Asian Americas* which was produced by the Asian American Filmmakers Collaborative (AAFC) in New York City. The challenge was to write a three-minute short film which featured Asian characters in New York and could be shot on digital video. I gave myself the added challenge of writing something which could work online—this was in 1999, after all, a year when everyone was trying to figure out how to make his or her fortune through the internet.

David Henry Hwang in *Asian Pride Porn*

After mulling these requirements, I came up with an infomercial spoof in which Tony Award winning playwright David Henry Hwang would hock progressive pornography featuring smart Asian women and sexually empowered Asian men. The infomercial and porn-spoof content justified shooting on video. The subject matter was totally appropriate for the Asian American anthology project and gave me practice in trying another tactic—satire—to challenge the misrepresentation of Asians in mainstream American media. And the fact that the film's title started with an "A" and included the word "porn" seemed like a sure route to online success.

Writing *Asian Pride Porn* also gave me the chance to flex a different set of muscles. While they included quirky situations and some laughs, *Mouse* and *Corporis Vesalius* were essentially dramas. *Asian Pride Porn*, on the other hand, was a broad satire packed with jokes. Making the film honed my comedy writing skills and in particular helped me understand how certain verbal gags need to be paired with visual gags for maximum impact. As readers may note, the script never describes any images of sex or skin. But when I showed the first cut of the film to the other members of the AAFC, it became clear that I needed to show *something* to pump up the visceral impact and help the jokes really go over. We shot a few scenes which showed a lot of skin (though no nudity) and through clever framing implied some ridiculous sexual positions. Boffo laffs ensued. Lesson learned.

Asian Pride Porn and its follow up bait-and-switch porn spoof, *All Amateur Ecstasy*, a one-joke, two-minute comedy which I can't really describe without spoiling the gag, played dozens of festivals and ended up at AtomFilms.com, where they've been among the site's most viewed films for years.

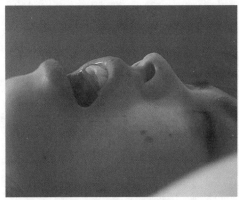

Sophia Skiles in *All Amateur Ecstasy*

Cat Fight Tonight, in which a psychotic couple fights over the custody of a cat, was the last of the digital shorts I made before directing my feature film Robot Stories. Aesthetically, I knew from the beginning that *Cat Fight Tonight* might be compromised. Cheap digital video was

Sophia Skiles in *Cat Fight Tonight*

the perfect choice for porn spoofs like *Asian Pride Porn* and *All Amateur Ecstasy*. In contrast, *Cat Fight Tonight* was a character-based narrative which would probably be better served by the more evocative textures of 16mm film. But by early 2001, I knew I would be shooting *Robot Stories* in the fall. And while I'd kept busy behind the camera with satires like *Asian Pride Porn*, I hadn't directed straight scenes with actors since *Mouse*. Thanks to the affordability of digital video, *Cat Fight Tonight* gave me the chance to tackle dramatic material again. The brief short also gave me another chance to play with badly behaving characters as heroes, something I'd explore further in *Robot Stories*.

ASIAN PRIDE PORN

FINAL DRAFT
November 22, 1999

FADE IN.

INT. LIVING ROOM - NIGHT

Tony Award winning playwright DAVID HENRY HWANG smiles at the camera.

> **DAVID**
>
> Hi. I'm David Henry Hwang. Most of you know me from my Tony Award winning play "M. Butterfly." But I'm here today to talk about something else altogether.

In classic infomercial style, David turns and we:

CUT TO a closer shot of him from a different angle.

> **DAVID (cont'd)**
>
> Porn.

He walks toward a television console.

> **DAVID (cont'd)**
>
> Now if you like pornography, you know all about "Asian" or "Oriental" porn.

David presses a button on a remote control.

ANGLE ON THE TELEVISION SCREEN:

A comely Asian PORN STAR gives the camera a come hither look as a 970 phone sex number flashes beneath her.

> **HUSKY FEMALE VOICE**
>
> Oriental Blossoms, where every flower's ripe for plucking.

> **PORN STAR**
>
> (with generic Asian accent)
>
> Give me a call. I'm waiting.

David turns to the camera and shakes his head.

DAVID

I just don't know. Sure, it'll do in a pinch, but when I'm lonely and bored, I don't need guilt over the sexual oppression of women of color and anger about the absence-slash-emasculation of the Asian male in American media to add to my shame of masturbation and societally-induced self-loathing. So imagine my happy surprise when I discovered...

He holds up a video box. The photo features a good-looking Asian man and woman embracing. The title reads:

"ASIAN PRIDE PORN"

DAVID (cont'd)

"Asian Pride Porn." Positive images of confident Asian American men and women caught on tape in the hottest hardcore action currently legal in North America!

INT. FOYER - NIGHT (SCENE FROM THE VIDEO)

An Asian American WOMAN in a business suit talks on the phone.

WOMAN

I don't know, Gloria. I guess I'm realizing that Reginald's just too... whitebread for me.

The BUZZER rings.

WOMAN (cont'd)

Whoops. Gotta go.

She opens the door to reveal a good-looking CHINESE DELIVERY MAN.

MAN

Hi. You ordered the...

(heavy with innuendo)

...Mongolian beef?

They lock eyes. Oooh, baby.

WOMAN

Hot and spicy.

MAN

Chinese home style.

He drops the package.

They embrace.

INT. LIVING ROOM - NIGHT

David smiles and nods.

DAVID

Smart Asian women, sexually-empowered Asian men? That's good politics.

GROANS and MOANS come from the television set.

David smiles.

DAVID (cont'd)

... and great porn.

He dims the lights and sits back on the couch to watch the television.

MAN (O.S.)

(on television)

Chow fun or ho fun?

WOMAN (O.S.)

Ho fun! Ho fun!

NARRATOR (V.O.)

Asian Pride Porn, available now in sex shops and community centers everywhere. Look for these new releases:

As the Narrator speaks each title, goofball cover art flashes across the screen.

NARRATOR (V.O.) (cont'd)

"Anna and the Kink," "Princess MonoNookie," and "Whole Lotta Hapa: the Eurasian Man-Meat Special," starring Dean "Candy" Cain and the Tilly Sisters.

(speaking very quickly)

Special discounts for students and seniors. All models and actors over 18 years of age. Not available in Georgia, Alabama, and certain parts of Flushing. All packages shipped discreetly in boxes marked, "Chinese American Voter Turnout in the Sacramento Municipal Elections, 1972-1976, Volume Four." Call now and you also get the full six hour uncut Pamela Anderson/Chow Yun Fat sex tapes.

Logos flash across the screen.

DAVID

From Onanism to Activism. Asian Pride Porn!

NARRATOR

Call today!

FADE TO BLACK.

END.

ALL | AMATEUR ECSTASY

FINAL DRAFT
March 1 , 2001

FADE IN.

INT. BEDROOM - DAY

Close up of a WOMAN lying in bed, eyes closed. She's flushed, disheveled, glorious and gorgeous. Her lips part. She inhales, then MOANS faintly.

INT. SHOWER - DAY

A SECOND WOMAN stands in the shower, surrounded by steam. She gasps for breath orgasmically.

INT. OFFICE - DAY

A THIRD WOMAN sits at her desk, holding a cup of coffee in her left hand. Her right hand is out of sight. She shudders and GROANS. The coffee trembles in her hand.

INT. BEDROOM - DAY

The First Woman's hand clutches her sheet as her ecstasy increases.

INT. SHOWER - DAY

The Second Woman's hand trembles in the air, surrounded by billowing steam as she MOANS.

INT. OFFICE - DAY

In the throes of ecstasy, the Third Woman blindly tries to set her mug down on the table but knocks it over with a HISS.

INT. BEDROOM - DAY

The First Woman gasps for air, peaking...

> **WOMAN 1**
>
> Oh my --

INT. SHOWER - DAY

> **WOMAN 2**
>
> Goodness, oh my --

INT. OFFICE - DAY

>   WOMAN 3
>
>   God --

INT. BEDROOM - DAY

The First Woman SNEEZES explosively.

INT. SHOWER - DAY

The Second Woman SNEEZES.

INT. OFFICE - DAY

The Third Woman SNEEZES.

INT. BEDROOM - DAY

The First Woman sits up in bed and blows her nose languorously.

>   **WOMAN**
>
>   Nice.

FADE TO BLACK.

END.

CAT FIGHT TONIGHT

FINAL DRAFT
April 22 , 2001

FADE IN.

EXT. APARTMENT - DAY

MIDGE, an unkempt young woman with an unhinged look in her eyes, peers at the door of a building across the street.

The door swings open.

Midge's lip curls into a snarl.

A sloppy young man named BUDDY exits the building, eating a banana.

> **MIDGE**
>
> That's right. Walk away. Walk the fuck away, you fucking fuck.

As soon as Buddy turns the corner, Midge marches across the street and heads up the stairs of the building.

She's holding a CAT CARRIER in one hand.

INT. APARTMENT - DAY

Keys turn in the locks and the door opens.

MIDGE enters the apartment.

She looks around.

> **MIDGE**
>
> Hey, Polly... Pollyanna...

A small orange CAT pads into the room and looks up at her.

> **MIDGE**
>
> Hello, baby!

Midge picks up the Cat and snuggles it with her face.

> **MIDGE**
>
> How you doing there, sweetie? You miss me? You miss me, sweetie? I missed you. You're the prettiest cat in the world, you know that? The prettiest little kitty --

The Cat GROWLS and jumps away.

Midge's eyes fall on a picture on the wall -- it's a photo of her and Buddy in each other's arms, grinning at the camera.

She scowls.

EXT. APARTMENT - DAY

Keys turn in the locks.

Buddy walks into the apartment, carrying a few bags of groceries.

> **BUDDY**
> (in a baby-talk voice)
>> Hey, Polly. Little Pollyanna.

He walks into the kitchen, disappearing from frame.

> **BUDDY (O.S.)**
>> Where's my little sweetie? Where's my pretty little kitty?

He walks back out of the kitchen, looking for the cat, and enters the bedroom.

> **BUDDY**
>> Polly?

He stares into the garbage can.

The framed photo of him and Midge lies in the garbage, the glass shattered.

Buddy snarls.

EXT. MIDGE'S APARTMENT - DAY

Midge exits her building and walks down the street.

ACROSS THE STREET,

Buddy glowers at her back.

> **BUDDY**
> (muttering)
>> You cannot touch me. And if you try I will eat you alive. I will flay the skin from your bones. I will --

Midge disappears around the corner. Buddy bolts for the building.

He's toting a CAT CARRIER in one hand.

INT. MIDGE'S APARTMENT - DAY

Midge enters the apartment, pulling a sack of cat food from a grocery bag.

MIDGE

Polly!

Nothing.

Midge's face changes.

On the table sits the photo of her and Buddy, now in a new frame. There's a mustache and beard drawn on her face.

MIDGE

Bastard!

INT. BUDDY'S APARTMENT - DAY

The keys turn in the lock.

Midge enters the apartment, cat carrier in hand.

MIDGE

Polly?

She walks into the kitchen.

She exits the kitchen and walks into the bedroom.

MIDGE

Polly?

No cat.

MIDGE

Goddammit.

QUICK SERIES OF CUTS:

Midge opens the oven.

Midge pushes aside the shower curtain.

Midge looks under the bed.

Midge peers under the desk.

BUDDY (O.S.)

Midge!

Midge bangs her head on the bottom of the desk.

MIDGE

Dammit!

Buddy stands over her.

BUDDY

Serves you right.

MIDGE

Burn in hell.

BUDDY

Yeah, yeah. Where's Polly?

MIDGE

What the fuck.

BUDDY

The cat!

MIDGE

You suck, Buddy. You suck so hard.

BUDDY

You suck a million times harder than me.

MIDGE

Than "I."

BUDDY

Whatever.

MIDGE

(imitating him)

Whatever.

BUDDY
(imitating her)

Whatever.

She shoves him. He grabs her arm as he stumbles backward. They fall together.

They stare at each other.

They kiss.

They tumble onto the bed.

They kiss deeply, pulling each other's clothes off.

She gasps, then laughs a little.

As they embrace,

ACROSS THE ROOM

The Cat sits on the floor gazing at the couple.

The Cat PURRS, blinking slowly, entirely contented.

FADE TO BLACK.

END.

4. RICE WORLD
introduction

During the years I was making no-budget digital shorts like *Asian Pride Porn* and *All Amateur Ecstasy*, I was simultaneously working on any good story idea I had, regardless of how impractical it might be in terms of actual production. I figured that the experience of writing would teach me something, and that if I wrote something really great, I'd eventually figure out how to make it.

Rice World, a mockumentary about an Asian American filmmaker who's assassinated after creating a series of controversial commercials for the rice industry, may be my favorite script in my folder of unproduced short screenplays. Like *Asian Pride Porn*, it uses satire to tackle issues of Asian stereotyping in American media. But it builds to a bittersweet ending which makes me smile in another way altogether.

RICE WORLD

FINAL DRAFT
September 2 , 2000

Rice World @ 2000 Greg Pak

FADE IN.

A PHOTOGRAPH of HORATIO KIM, an earnest young Asian American filmmaker holding a movie camera, fills the screen.

> **ANNOUNCER (V.O.)**
>
> In October 1996, independent filmmaker Horatio Kim was offered the job of making a series of promotional commercials for the National Rice Appreciation Association.

IN A PHOTO, a group of smiling WHITE BUSINESSMEN stand around a big rice bag bearing the logo of the National Rice Appreciation Association.

> **ANNOUNCER (V.O.)**
>
> At first, Horatio made a big deal of rejecting the offer.

CLOSE UP of the turning spool in a Nagra tape recorder.

> **HORATIO (V.O.)**
>
> Look, Mom, the scripts are just... embarrassing. I don't think it's right.

> **MOM (V.O.)**
>
> Honey, whatever you do, we'll be proud of you.

A grainy, blown-up SURVEILLANCE PHOTOGRAPH of Horatio on the street fills the screen.

> **ANNOUNCER (V.O.)**
>
> In the end, the National Rice Appreciation Association doubled its offer, and Horatio took the job.

In close detail of another PHOTOGRAPH, a tall WHITE MAN presses a fat, manila envelope into Horatio's hands.

INT. STUDIO - DAY

A distinguished-looking ANNOUNCER turns to the camera.

> **ANNOUNCER**
>
> We've all followed the nationwide controversy, which began with the broadcast of Horatio's first commercial on Pearl Harbor Day, 1997, and ended with Horatio's tragic demise two years later. But few know that

Horatio's final Rice Appreciation Association ad never even aired. Here for the first time are all of the commercials in the series. Perhaps by looking at the entire campaign, we can begin to understand this tormented figure so reviled by his own community.

INT. CHINESE RESTAURANT - DAY (RICE COMMERCIAL 1)

A group of NON-ASIAN PEOPLE sit around the table, trying with little success to pick up rice with their chopsticks.

> **ANNOUNCER 2**
>
> Ever get frustrated trying to eat in a Chinese restaurant? How the heck do they pick up that dry, flaky Chinese rice with those slippery plastic chopsticks?

INT. HOUSE - DAY

A happy Chinese family eats dinner at home.

> **ANNOUNCER 2**
>
> Well, at home, Chinese people eat sticky rice that holds together nicely for easy chopstick handling!

IN CLOSE UP, a pair of chopsticks neatly lifts a clump of sticky rice.

> **ANNOUNCER 2**
>
> Try REAL CHINESE PEOPLE'S RICE, a new product developed by the National Rice Appreciation Association.

The Non-Asian People from the first scene beam at the camera, cheerfully eating sticky rice with chopsticks.

> **ANNOUNCER 2**
>
> Complimentary wooden chopsticks included in each box.

INT. BURGER RESTAURANT - DAY

ARCHIBALD, an Asian American teenager, face wrenched with emotion, sits at a table.

ARCHIBALD

I was riding my bike home from school when this pack of kids attacked me...

INTERVIEWER

White kids?

ARCHIBALD

Mostly. There was a Japanese kid, too. They were all yelling, throwing chopsticks. They'd just seen the commercial, I guess. They kept saying, "Where's the sticky rice, Archibald? Where's the sticky rice?"

Archibald breaks down and sobs.

ANNOUNCER (V.O.)

After viewing the commercial, millions of Americans became convinced there was a Chinese conspiracy to humiliate diners with intentionally dry rice.

EXT. CHINESE RESTAURANT - DAY (NEWS FOOTAGE)

A crowd of people chants and shouts, waving signs with slogans like, "MAKE IT STICKY, STINKY!" and "WE'RE ONTO YOU, WONG!"

ANNOUNCER (V.O.)

But in sad truth, many Chinese American families eat dry, flaky rice at home. Chinese kids across the country were scarred forever by demands for "sticky rice" that they simply didn't understand.

INT. BURGER RESTAURANT - DAY

Archibald stares down sadly at a hamburger and fries.

ANNOUNCER (V.O.)

Some, like Archibald Chow, have been unable to eat rice ever since.

INT. HOUSE - DAY

Horatio's MOM and DAD sit side by side on the couch.

DAD

The phone started ringing right away.

MOM

People said the most terrible things. They called us bananas.

DAD

Twinkies.

MOM

Uncle Tongs.

INTERVIEWER (O.S)

How did you feel about the commercial?

DAD

Well, he said he had no control over the script or anything.

MOM

He said the next one would be better.

(beat)

He said it would make us proud.

Dad sighs ruefully.

INT. KITCHEN - DAY (RICE COMMERCIAL 2)

JOHNNY, a white boy, and MICHAEL, an Asian boy, sit at the table doing homework while Johnny's MOM dries dishes.

Johnny throws down his pencil in frustration.

JOHNNY

I can't do this trig!

MOM

"Can't" means "won't," honey.

> **MICHAEL**
>
> Come on, it's not that hard...

Mom gazes at the boys, a concerned expression on her face.

> **MOM (V.O.)**
>
> Johnny tries so hard... How come it comes so easy for Michael?

> **MICHAEL**
>
> Say, I'm starting to get fuzzy in the head. How 'bout a snack?

Michael pulls a bowl of rice from his lunch box.

Mom's eyes widen: AHA!

INT. KITCHEN - NEXT DAY

Johnny and Michael run into the room excitedly, waving test papers.

> **JOHNNY**
>
> Hey, Mom! I got an A!

Mom smiles knowingly and presents two steaming bowls of rice.

> **MICHAEL**
>
> (winking at Johnny)
>
> I told you it wasn't so hard!

All share a laugh as the boys start eating.

> **ANNOUNCER 2 (V.O.)**
>
> Rice. Their little secret. A message from the National Rice Appreciation Association.

INT. OFFICE - DAY

ADELINA TANAKA and FREMONT OHARA, Field Directors of the Asian American Protest League, sit grimly in front of a banner reading "KIM IS A BIG ASS."

> **TANAKA**
>
> After that second ad, we had no choice.

EXT. HORATIO'S APARTMENT - DAY (NEWS FOOTAGE)

Horatio walks out of his apartment. A line of ASIAN AMERICAN PROTESTORS hold signs with arrows pointing to him. The signs read "PUNK," "DUMBASS," and " SELF-HATING PERPETUATOR OF STEREOTYPES ABOUT HIS OWN PEOPLE."

> **OHARA (V.O.)**
>
> We started picketing twenty four seven.

INT. HORATIO'S APARTMENT - NIGHT (NEWS FOOTAGE)

Horatio sits inside his apartment, watching television. Protestors sit on either side of him, still holding their signs, also watching television.

> **INTERVIEWER (V.O.)**
>
> But what's so terrible about depicting Asians as academic achievers?

INT. OFFICE - DAY

Tanaka and Ohara sneer at the off-screen Interviewer.

> **OHARA**
>
> Come on, all this "model minority" talk is just a load of horseshit carted around by conservative politicians trying to avoid responsibility for the nation's woefully inadequate public education and social service structures.

> **TANAKA**
>
> But what really galled us was that he attributed our success to what we *eat*.

> **OHARA**
>
> As if high scores in math depended on the consumption of the products of corporate American factory farming.

> **TANAKA**
>
> Rather than basic cultural superiority.

> **OHARA**
>
> Yeah! What?

ANNOUNCER (V.O.)

In spite of the protesters, or perhaps because of them, Kim kept going.

EXT. CITY HALL - DAY

Horatio stands behind a podium, surrounded by CAMERA CREWS, REPORTERS, and PROTESTORS.

HORATIO

You may not like what I say, but you should defend to your death my right to say it!

The Protesters rush the podium.

HORATIO

Shit.

Horatio flees.

HORATIO (V.O.)

All I ever wanted to do was bring people closer together.

Recorded on jerky, handheld video, the crowd chases Horatio through the street.

HORATIO (V.O.)

I guess people don't really wanna get any closer together.

INT./EXT. FRONT DOOR - DAY (RICE COMMERCIAL 3)

A forty-something WHITE MOM opens the front door to reveal her beaming white daughter, MARCIA.

MARCIA

Hey, Mom! Meet Richard!

RICHARD, Marcia's ASIAN BOYFRIEND, steps into frame.

MARCIA

We're starved! What's for dinner?

A worried look crosses Mom's face.

MOM (V.O.)

What'll he think of my *rice*...

INT. DINING ROOM - EVENING

Richard dredges up a polite smile while forcing a forkful of flaky, dry rice into his mouth.

RICHARD

Mmmm, it's great, Mrs. Smythe.

Mom smiles, terribly embarrassed.

RICHARD

Hey, Marcia... Maybe I can't make that party after all...

Marcia's face falls.

INT. KOREAN GROCERY - DAY

A KOREAN GROCER grins at the camera and pulls a bag of rice from the shelf.

GROCER

Korean boyfriend? You need Korean rice! Steam up nice and sticky, perfect for eating with chopsticks, but so simple to use, even white people can make it!

INT. DINING ROOM - THE NEXT DAY

Richard tucks into a perfect bowl of steaming rice.

RICHARD

Now *this* is *rice*!

Mom and Marcia beam at each other.

Church bells GONG.

EXT. CHURCH - DAY

Marcia and Richard run down the steps of the church as Mom and the Korean Grocer throw rice from the special bag.

ANNOUNCER

Rice. Now it's for all of us. A message from the National Rice Appreciation Association.

INT. PARK - DAY (HANDHELD HOME VIDEO FOOTAGE)

Horatio stands at a podium, speaking at an Asian arts festival to a crowd of surly activists, dragon dancers, and tai-chi demonstrators.

HORATIO

So what's so terrible about recognizing difference, and recognizing similarities, and saying, what the hell, I *am* attracted to that white woman. I *do* --

GUNFIRE splits the air.

Horatio keels sideways.

Mayhem as the camera pans and swerves.

FREEZE FRAME on MRS. HWANG, a middle-aged Korean mother perched in a tree with a rifle in her hands.

INT. NEWS STUDIO - DAY

A NEWSCASTER talks as images of Mrs. HWANG flash behind him.

NEWSCASTER

And in a stunning twist, Channel Seven has learned that Mrs. Hwang was the mother of an actor in Kim's last commercial.

EXT. HOUSE - DAY

The actor who played RICHARD, his arm around the actress who played MARCIA, faces a crowd of shouting camera crews.

RICHARD

We loved each other on camera -- and in real life! Is that so wrong?

INT. PRISON - DAY

Mrs. Hwang, in a prisoner's orange jumpsuit, sits behind the glass of a visitation booth.

MRS. HWANG

(completely unrepentant)

Yes.

EXT. CEMETARY - DAY

News footage of Ohara and Tanaka hammering "BURN IN HELL" and "RACE TRAITOR" signs alongside Horatio's fresh grave.

EXT. STREET - NIGHT

Crowds of Asian Americans roam the street, cheering, laughing, and celebrating.

EXT. PARK - DAY

The Announcer walks along a grassy ridge in the park.

ANNOUNCER

Perhaps Horatio deserved the assassin's bullet that felled him. Perhaps all the positive messages he tried to instill in his rice appreciation ads could not offset the terrible wounds he inflicted upon the soul of Asian America. But before we judge, perhaps we should view Horatio's final work, the never-before broadcast "Rice World" ad.

DISSOLVE TO:

EXT. PARK - DAY (RICE WORLD COMMERCIAL)

A lovely grassy slope, framed against a sky blue sky.

A small Asian TOT appears over the edge of the slope. The camera moves forward as the Tot SINGS.

TOT

In a world full of strife,

Of struggle and pain

Sometimes it's hard to see

The sun through the rain.

But when people 'round the world

Sit down for a hot lunch,

There's a humble little grain

Upon which we all munch.

As the camera rises, the Tot lifts a steaming bowl of RICE.

A dozen PEOPLE of all races and cultures, dressed in traditional costumes and holding plates and bowls of their native rice-based dishes, appear behind the Tot.

ALL

Rice, rice, rice.

Won't you join us in our song?

Rice, rice, rice

Can't we all just get along?

KOREAN

In Seoul it's in kim bab

JAPANESE

It's in sushi in Tokyo

ENGLISHWOMAN

I need it for my Christmas pudding

CAJUN

I put it een mah gumbo

INDIAN

Without rice, who'd eat masala?

MEXICAN

My refried beans would taste so lame

JAMAICAN

My chicken jerk would just be jerky

ALL

We all need rice – we're all the same.

The camera swirls and rises – there's a long spiral of people, all singing together, smiling at each other, proffering each other their various native dishes.

ALL

Rice, rice, rice.

Won't you join us in our song?

Rice, rice, rice

Horatio beams beatifically at the camera, dressed like the little Tot at the beginning of the commercial, holding up a simple bowl of rice.

HORATIO

Can't we all just get along?

Freeze frame.

SUPERIMPOSED TITLE:

Horatio Kim

1973 - 1999

END.

5. ROBOT STORIES
introduction

Origins

Ray Bradbury was my first hero. I loved Bradbury for writing about rockets, Martians, robots, and dinosaurs while always finding the tiny human details which made his stories so compelling. I was a fan of the *Twilight Zone*, Marvel Comics, *High Noon*, *Seven Samurai*, and *Jaws* for the same reasons—all involve stories whose genre elements become all the more powerful because of the emotional honesty of their characters' struggles. So when I started writing and directing films of my own, I had an ingrained inclination to pair intimate human stories with strong genre elements. *Random Man* was a superhero story. *Corporis Vesalius* was a period costume drama. Even *Mouse* had a touch of monster movie in it.

Genre writing had an added attraction for me as an Asian American filmmaker. I'd always been compelled by the potential power of movies to break down stereotypes. And given the dearth of three-dimensional roles for Asian Americans on the big screen, I'd consistently written Asian American protagonists into my screenplays. Occasionally colleagues would suggest that casting Asian Americans might limit the ability of the projects to reach wide audiences. I'd point to Spike Lee's adage that the more specific something is, the more universal it can become. It's precisely those specific details of a character's background which give his or her story authenticity and make it believable and accessible to people everywhere. My small successes with *Mouse* and *Fighting Grandpa* seemed to demonstrate the point. But at the same time, I knew that many people—both Asian and non-Asian—had an automatic bias against Asian American films. They assumed that an Asian American movie would be an earnest message movie, a film they *should* see but didn't necessarily *want* to see. Genre seemed like a perfect tool to apply to the problem.

Asian Pride Porn was evidence that an esoteric discussion about racial represen-tation in mainstream media could get a big audience when combined with satire and porn-spoofing. In a similar way, a story with Asian American protagonists might get a much wider audience if it happened to include genre hooks like aliens or androids. Furthermore, genre elements could provide new ways to evoke deeper consideration of social or political questions. Bradbury's *Martian Chronicles* is not only a tremendous genre adventure story and a moving series of vignettes about the human heart—but also a subtle exploration and condem-nation of imperialism, colonization, and genocide. Political subtext, emotional story, and genre inventiveness can work hand in hand, each enriching the other and drawing wider audiences as a result.

So over the years I played with many different genres, writing several horror screenplays with Asian American protagonists as well as *Rio Chino*, a straight up Western featuring a Chinese gunslinger and a Mexican heroine in the Old West. Unfortunately, all of these screenplays required budgets too large for me to pull together as a first-time feature filmmaker. So I kept making shorts and kept writ-ing, trying to come up with a genuinely low-budget script which could launch me into feature filmmaking.

While digging through my old files one day, I rediscovered several shorts I'd writ-ten over the years which shared certain themes. Each was about the length of a *Twilight Zone* episode, each told an emotionally resonant story in which characters grapple with a key, life-changing moment, and each featured robots or artificial intelligence. Making them as individual films was out—the market for shorts was-n't good enough to justify the investment. But if I could pull the stories together as an anthology film, the project might just work as a low-budget feature.

The four stories which eventually became my feature film *Robot Stories* included "Machine Love," in which an android office worker learns that he, too, needs love; "The Robot Fixer," in which a mother becomes obsessed with completing her dying son's robot toy collection; "My Robot Baby," in which a couple who

Robot Stories theatrical release poster

want to adopt a human child must first prove their parenting skills by taking care of a robot baby; and "Clay," in which an old sculptor must choose between natural death and digital immortality.

Like Mouse, the stories followed the improviser's principle of fully exploring one quirky idea. Like *Mouse* and *Cat Fight Tonight*, the stories further explored the notion that badly behaving characters may be the most interesting. And like *Rio Chino* and my other feature screenplays, the stories would let me test the strategy of using genre to win a wider audience for stories with Asian American protagonists. Finally, using its genre potential to explore deeper political themes, the film could almost subliminally challenge the way both Asians and robots are frequently stereotyped as inhuman, emotionless, hyper-efficient aliens.

The question now was how to make the stories work together as an anthology film.

Developing the Anthology

From the beginning, it was clear that the four tales of *Robot Stories* had thematic similarities. But shared themes wouldn't guarantee the four stories would work together as a feature. For the feature to be satisfying, the stories needed to build, each leading to the next emotional moment so that when the movie ended, the audience would walk away having had a complete experience. We needed to figure out the feature's larger story.

During script development, producer Kim Ima and I brainstormed about having main characters in one story appear as minor characters in others. Perhaps we could create subtle through-lines so that the combined experiences of the characters would build into a single emotional super-story of the struggle to connect at different stages in a person's life.

The network of links we developed began by connecting the emotional lives of Archie, the android hero of "Machine Love," and John, the main character of "Clay." In "Machine Love," Archie observes John and his wife Helen experiencing an emotional crisis on the subway. Archie draws on the memory later as he tries to sort through his own experiences of loneliness and alienation. Much later, in "Clay," John struggles as an old man with the emotional disconnection from his wife which was hinted at in the "Machine Love" scene. But now Archie makes a cheerful cameo on John's train. Earlier, John taught Archie about human sadness. Now Archie, having experienced life on his own, provides John with a subtle, silent counter-argument. Maybe John has it all wrong; maybe tragedy isn't inevitable; maybe he should embrace love wherever he can find it. The characters feed into each other's stories and challenge each other to reach the next level.

Similar links connect the other stories. In "Machine Love," Marcia is a heartless office flirt and Bernice is a harsh office manager whose actions help precipitate Archie's emotional meltdown. Later, Bernice and Marcia return as the main characters of their own stories and experience emotional crises which echo Archie's experience. Small details help remind us of the links. Bernice has trouble relating to the G9 iPerson Archie in "Machine Love": later, in "Robot Fixer," we learn that Bernice's estranged son, whom she never understood, is called "the G9" by his coworkers. Archie's coworkers turn off the lights, leaving him alone in the dark office, just as Marcia's mother later leaves Marcia alone in a dark closet.

With producers Kim Ima and Karin Chien, cinematographer Peter Olsen, a talented crew, and a tremendous cast which included veterans such as Tamlyn Tomita, Sab Shimono, and Wai Ching Ho, we shot *Robot Stories* in the fall of 2001 and premiered it at the Hamptons International Film Festival a year later. The film eventually screened at 75 film festivals, won 35 awards, toured the country in a city-by-city theatrical release, and is now available on DVD from Kino International.

Photo by Wesley Law

Director Greg Pak and actor Tamlyn Tomita

It would be nice to assume that our subtle links between stories cracked the code for our anthology picture, pulling the struggles of our individual characters into an emotional story greater than the sum of its parts. But many of the links never made it to the final film. Scheduling problems didn't allow us to have the same actress play the office flirt in "Machine Love" and Marcia in "My Robot Baby." Similar problems kept Helen out of the opening scene of "Machine Love" and compromised the Archie cameo in "Clay."

Ultimately, the challenge of making the stories come together as a feature had to be addressed once again in the editing room.

The Script Versus the Film

In the *Robot Stories* shooting script which follows, "Machine Love" is the first story, followed by "The Robot Fixer," "My Robot Baby," and "Clay." The order made sense at the time we shot. Rhythmically and tonally, it felt right to have the lightest film lead, followed by a heavier film, followed by a lighter story, and ending with the heaviest and most open-ended of the tales. On a character level, the order made sense as well—we'd start with Archie, a fresh-faced innocent at the beginning of his life, and conclude with John, a weary, raging man facing his death.

But in post-production, editor Stephanie Sterner gradually came to realize that there might be a better arrangement. In the final film, "Machine Love" and "My Robot Baby" swapped places. That simple switch helped create much more coherent chronological and thematic arcs for the whole movie. Now the progression of technology made sense—the science began with the clunky robot baby, developed into the android Archie, and ended with the super-advanced implementation of digital immortality. As a result, the world of the movie became more coherent and believable. Similarly, the thematic thread connecting the stories finally clicked. Progressing from a baby to an old man made it much clearer that our characters shared an emotional story spanning an allegorical life cycle.

Readers may enjoy exploring other differences between the shooting script and the final film. For example, the "Clay" segment of the screenplay involves a subplot in which our sculptor hero is pursued by agents intent upon forcing him to be scanned. The scenes provide dramatic tension and a deeper understanding of the paranoid political world of "Clay." But due to scheduling problems, we had to drop the subplot from the final film and restructure the entire segment. Yet sometimes on-set disasters can be a blessing in disguise. In this case, omitting the subplot forced us to concentrate on the relationship between Helen and John, ultimately strengthening the emotional impact of the film.

Director Greg Pak and actor Sab Shimono

Photo by Wesley Law

The shooting script also includes alternate endings which provide a glimpse into Marcia's next step with her mechanical tot in "My Robot Baby" and a deeper exploration of the bittersweet perfection of the scanning experience in "Clay." Cutting these scenes from the final film was a tough decision—I was particularly fond of the twist at the end of "Clay," which could have worked beautifully if the film had been a stand-alone short. But as the last story in a feature length anthology, "Clay" would bring all of our characters' emotional stories to a close. Cutting the twist kept the focus on John's human struggle and maintained the integrity of the emotional journey we were striving to trace through all of our characters' lives.

ROBOT STORIES

FINAL SHOOTING SCRIPT
September 5 , 2001

TITLE CARD: MACHINE LOVE

FADE IN.

INT. SUBWAY - DAY

Lights flash by, illuminating the face of:

ARCHIE, a pale young man in khakis and a blue Oxford, who sits inside the subway, unnaturally erect and wide-eyed.

A sharp BREATH hits the air.

Archie turns to see:

JOHN and HELEN, a young man and woman, sitting on the other side of the car. John slouches, drawn and pale, as if he hasn't slept for days. Helen sits beside him, speaking quietly into his ear.

John's face wrenches up, then relaxes. Then wrenches up again. He covers his eyes with one hand.

The subway's brakes SCREECH.

John lets out a SOB.

> **JOHN**
>
> Oh, Jesus.

John WEEPS.

Helen looks away.

Archie stares, expressionless. His lips move slightly, silently mouthing "Oh, Jesus."

A COMMUTER crosses in front of Archie. Archie turns to watch as the Commuter pulls open the door and passes to the next car.

For a brief moment, Archie locks eyes with LYDIA, a pale young woman in a blue Oxford sitting in the adjoining car.

They stare at each other through the windows, wide-eyed and blank-faced.

The train lurches to a stop.

Archie blinks.

Lydia is gone.

Archie turns to stare at the open doors of the subway.

EXT. STREET/OFFICE BUILDING - DAY

Archie walks down the street. His movements are stiff but precise. He turns and walks up the steps of a large office building.

INT. RECEPTIONIST'S DESK - DAY

The RECEPTIONIST looks up as Archie steps forward. He hands her some paperwork and a fat manila envelope.

His face remains blank, but his voice has a user-friendly cheerfulness.

> **ARCHIE**
>
> Hello. My name is Archie.

She glances at the paperwork, then looks back up at Archie with interest. She presses an office intercom button and leans forward, eyes still on Archie.

> **RECEPTIONIST**
>
> The Coder's here.

INT. ARCHIE'S CUBICLE/MAIN OFFICE - DAY

BERNICE, the office manager, points Archie toward a computer crammed into a corner in the hallway next to the photocopier and water cooler.

> **ARCHIE**
>
> It's a pleasure to be here. I look forward to our interactions. The more --

> **BERNICE**
>
> This is your space. Your first assignments should already be listed there.

> **ARCHIE**
>
> Very good.

Bernice, the Receptionist, and a few other Office Workers watch as Archie wedges himself into the chair in front of the computer. He swivels to gaze at them.

> **ARCHIE (cont'd)**
>
> The more we interact, the more I can tailor my work to your expectations. I hope --

BERNICE

My only expectations are that you get the work done. So why don't you get started?

Archie blinks.

ARCHIE

Very good.

The Workers exchange glances.

Archie turns to the screen. He stares for an instant, then begins to type at an incredible pace.

A pleasant machine CHIME comes from across the room.

VOICE

(from across the office)

Hey, my system's back up!

BOB, the chubby, sweaty tech guy, grins as he walks forward.

BOB

He just delivered himself?

RECEPTIONIST

Yep.

BOB

Awesome.

Bob pulls a manual from the envelope. The title reads:

The Sprout G9 iPerson

User's Manual

Archie types away, face blank.

INT. BERNICE'S OFFICE - DAY

Bernice sits in her office, playing Pac Man on her computer.

A faint CLICK hits the air.

She turns and jerks with surprise:

ARCHIE is standing behind her.

> **BERNICE**
>
> Oh my God.

> **ARCHIE**
>
> I have completed all of my assigned tasks.

> **BERNICE**
>
> Okay. Go back and sit down. We'll send you some more work soon.

> **ARCHIE**
>
> Thank you.

(beat)

> Would you like me to address you as Bernice or Ms. Chin?

> **BERNICE**
>
> Go sit down.

> **ARCHIE**
>
> Very good.

Archie turns and walks away.

Bernice pushes the button on the intercom on her desk.

> **BERNICE**
>
> Bob, come in here.

INT. MAIN OFFICE/ARCHIE'S CUBICLE - DAY

Bob, hunched slightly with trepidation, walks into Bernice's office and pulls the door shut.

The muffled sound of Bernice's sharp voice rises into the air.

On the other side of the office, Archie sits motionless in his chair, staring at the empty computer screen.

MARCIA, an attractive young woman, walks past.

Archie turns to see Marcia standing beside LARRY, another office worker, at the water cooler.

ARCHIE

Hello. My name is --

LARRY

Shut up. Turn around.

ARCHIE

Very good.

Archie turns away.

Marcia giggles.

MARCIA

Hey, you.

Archie turns toward her.

MARCIA (cont'd)

Turn around.

Archie turns away.

MARCIA (cont'd)

Hey.

Archie turns toward her.

MARCIA (cont'd)

Turn around.

Archie turns away.

MARCIA (cont'd)

Hey.

Archie turns toward her.

MARCIA (cont'd)

(to Larry)

Very obedient. I like that in a man.

LARRY

I dunno about that.

MARCIA

What do you know?

Larry looks around. No one's in sight. Bernice's VOICE continues to drone from behind her closed office door.

Larry hooks a finger into Marcia's blouse, then pulls her close.

Archie turns away.

Marcia giggles. She and Larry kiss.

Archie watches their reflection in the corner of his computer screen.

Archie's computer flickers and BEEPS.

He jerks slightly and his fingers begin to fly over the keyboard with a CLATTER.

Startled, Marcia and Larry pull out of their embrace. They stare at Archie's back as he types.

MARCIA (cont'd)

Freaky.

They laugh and walk down the hallway.

Archie's fingers continue typing, but his eyes follow Larry and Marcia.

Bob exits Bernice's office as Larry and Marcia pass.

Bob smiles shyly at Marcia and raises a hand.

Larry points at Bob's chest. Bob looks down. Larry lifts his hand and flicks Bob's nose. Marcia laughs.

BOB

(humiliated)

Ha, ha, very funny.

Bob sits down next to Archie.

BOB (cont'd)

How you doing there, Archie?

Archie hits the ENTER key and stops typing.

ARCHIE

Very well, thank you. I have completed all of my assigned tasks.

BOB

Yeah, I heard. Look, you gotta not creep up on people like that. If you have a question, find me.

ARCHIE

Very good.

Bob huffs on an inhaler.

ARCHIE (cont'd)

Should I address you as Mr. MacKedrick or Bob?

Bob gazes at Archie, then shakes his head and pages through the manual in his lap.

BOB

Look, I know you're designed to interact and adapt and all. But I don't think anyone here's really into that. People don't quite get you.

Beat.

ARCHIE

Freaky.

Bob stares at him.

Marcia's GIGGLE hits the air.

Bob looks up, then looks back down.

BOB

Yeah. Freaky.

Bob sighs.

BOB (cont'd)

You can call me Bob.

> **ARCHIE**
>
> All right, Bo --

Bob presses a button on the back of Archie's neck.

Archie's eyes close and his head tilts forward.

BLACK.

The welcoming START UP CHIME of a computer hits the air.

INT. ARCHIE'S CUBICLE/MAIN OFFICE - MORNING

Archie's eyes open.

> **ARCHIE**
>
> Good morning!

> **BERNICE**
>
> We're not going to hear <u>that</u> every day.

> **BOB**
>
> You got that, Archie?

> **ARCHIE**
>
> Very good.

Archie's computer BEEPS.

Archie turns to the computer screen in front of him and begins to type.

Bernice nods approvingly.

> **BERNICE**
>
> (to Bob)
>
> I'd like to see <u>you</u> working like that.

Bob forces a smile and backs away to his cubicle.

FROM ARCHIE'S POV:

Numbers whip across the screen and people zip through the office in FAST MOTION.

Archie stops typing and hits ENTER.

People move through the office in SLOW MOTION.

Archie watches them as they pass.

Bob approaches. He raises a hand and smiles. Archie starts to raise his hand in response. But Bob's not looking at Archie -- he's trying to catch Marcia's eye.

Marcia walks past behind Archie.

She turns away, avoiding Bob's gaze.

Bob lowers his hand, embarrassed.

Archie lowers his hand.

A BEEP hits the air. Archie's eyes flick to the screen and he resumes typing.

The people fly by in FAST MOTION.

He presses ENTER and stops typing.

Bob presses the back of Archie's neck.

BLACK.

START UP CHIME.

Archie's eyes open and he types furiously.

In the edge of his screen, he sees a reflection of Bob talking with Marcia.

People whip by in FAST MOTION.

Bob presses the back of Archie's neck.

BLACK.

START UP CHIME.

Archie types furiously.

BLACK.

START UP CHIME.

Archie types furiously, then hits ENTER.

The overhead lights go out.

Marcia's LAUGH hits the air.

Bob, eager and excited, follows Marcia and a few other employees outside, pulling the door shut behind them.

Archie sits at his desk in the dark, still powered up.

Archie blinks.

He looks over his shoulder.

The office is empty.

He turns back to his computer screen.

It's blank.

INT. OFFICE - NIGHT - BOB'S CUBICLE

Archie peers into the cubicle.

> **ARCHIE**
>
> Bob?

No one's there.

He turns to the dark, empty office.

> **ARCHIE**
>
> I have completed all of my assigned tasks.

INT./EXT. ARCHIE'S WINDOW - NIGHT

Archie walks past the window, turning slightly to gaze out.

He pulls up short.

In the window of an office across the street, a WOMAN in a blue Oxford sits at a desk.

It's LYDIA, the woman from the subway platform.

She types with blinding speed, gazing blankly at her computer screen.

A couple of MEN walk into the room. One of them is named ROY.

As Archie watches, the Men laugh and joke, pushing each other as they approach Lydia.

They sit on the desktop on either side of her.

Lydia hits ENTER and stops typing. She stares into space.

Roy slides a hand along her cheek.

The other Man eases a hand into her blouse.

Archie stares.

Lydia turns to gaze out the window.

Her eyes meet Archie's.

They stare at each other, blankly.

Julienne Hanzelka Kim in "Machine Love"

Her computer screen flickers.

She turns and resumes typing.

The Men laugh and back away from the desk.

INT. ARCHIE'S WINDOW - MORNING

Bob walks into the office and turns on the lights.

Archie lies on the floor by the window.

> **BOB**
>
> Oh, boy.

INT. OFFICE - BOB'S CUBICLE - DAY

The startup CHIME sounds.

Archie's eyes open.

He's sitting in Bob's cubicle. His shirt is off. Cables run from sockets on his back. He's plugged into the electrical socket on the wall.

> **BOB**
>
> What were you wandering around for?

> **ARCHIE**
>
> I was looking for you, Bob.

> **BOB**
>
> Well, ol' Bob wasn't here, was he? He was out with the big kids.

> **ARCHIE**
>
> Big kids?

Bob chuckles as he fiddles with the panel on Archie's back.

> **BOB**
>
> Yeah. It's like high school all over again. Buncha jerks. But if you get invited, you go. Buy her a drink, make a little small talk. Laying the groundwork, baby.

Bob grins, snapping the panel back into place.

BOB

You see, life's not just about work, Archie. Sometimes you gotta live a little.

Bernice pokes her head into the cubicle.

BERNICE

Everything okay?

BOB

Yeah. His batteries just ran out.

BERNICE

Just leave him plugged in.

Greg Pak and Bill Coelius in "Machine Love"

Photo by Wesley Law

INT. ARCHIE'S CUBICLE/MAIN OFFICE - DAY

Archie sits in his space, typing away.

But now he's shirtless. The cable which runs from his back is plugged into the wall.

The Receptionist stares at Archie's back as she makes copies.

Marcia walks up beside her.

RECEPTIONIST

You know, he's got a pretty nice build.

MARCIA

Like Ken. Ken had fantastic shoulders.

Marcia steps forward and runs her fingers along Archie's back, grinning over her shoulder at the Receptionist.

MARCIA

Rrrrow!

They laugh.

Archie keeps typing. But his eyes focus on the corner of his computer screen, where he watches the reflection of Marcia's hands squeezing his shoulder.

His eyes flick toward the window through which he saw Lydia.

INT. ARCHIE'S CUBICLE/MAIN OFFICE - EVENING

It's late -- the office is almost empty.

Bob talks on a cell phone, watching as Archie types.

> **BOB**
> (into the phone)
>> Yes, hello? Marcia? I can't hear you very well. So which bar did you --
>> Hello?
> (to Archie)
>> How much longer?

> **ARCHIE**
>> Two hours, thirteen minutes, seven seconds.

Bob glances at his watch.

> **BOB**
>> Damn.
> (into the phone)
>> No, no, no. I'll be there in half an hour. Okay? You guys'll still be --
>> Okay. Hello? Bye.
> (to Archie)
>> Okay, Archie. I'm leaving you on. Be a good boy, huh?

> **ARCHIE**
>> Yes, Bob.

Bob turns and leaves.

INT./EXT. ARCHIE'S WINDOW - NIGHT

Archie stands at the window, gazing down at the office across the street.

The lights are on, but no one's there.

From the back of the office, the sound of the DOOR opening and a woman's GIGGLE hit the air.

Archie turns to see a pair of silhouettes flit across the floor.

LARRY (O.S.)

Whoa, tiger --

MARCIA (O.S.)

Come on --

GIGGLES, SHUFFLING, and MURMURS.

Archie turns back to the window.

IN THE OFFICE ACROSS THE STREET,

A WOMAN enters the room, walking to the desk, gesturing toward someone who's still out of sight.

Archie leans forward slightly.

LYDIA walks into view.

Archie's mouth opens, then closes.

From the back of the office comes a MOAN followed by soft LAUGHTER.

IN THE OFFICE ACROSS THE STREET,

Lydia sits down at the desk and begins to type.

The Woman leaves the room and turns out the light.

Archie blinks.

Lydia types, her blank face illuminated by the computer screen.

Archie raises a hand.

From the back of the office, rhythmic SQUEAKING becomes audible.

Archie stands, frozen for a second...

... then taps on the glass.

Lydia continues to type.

The SQUEAKING becomes more intense.

Archie taps on the glass again.

Lydia just types.

Archie's face wrenches, then returns to normal.

Archie taps the glass again.

The SQUEAKING reaches a peak, followed by a CLATTER and Marcia's breathless LAUGHTER.

Lydia abruptly stops typing.

Archie starts.

Lydia stares into space.

Lydia stands, disappearing into darkness.

Archie stares.

Lydia reappears at the window.

Archie pounds on the glass.

> **LARRY (O.S.)**
>
> What the hell...

Lydia looks up.

Archie's computer BEEPS.

Archie turns to stare at his cubbyhole.

INT. LYDIA'S OFFICE - NIGHT

Lydia stares up into the night.

Archie's window is empty.

INT. ARCHIE'S CUBICLE/MAIN OFFICE - NIGHT

Archie sits at his desk, typing at his computer.

> **MARCIA (O.S.)**
>
> It's just the Coder.

Archie's face remains blank as ever, but there's a terrible tension building behind his eyes.

His face trembles.

INT. SUBWAY - DAY (ARCHIE'S MEMORY)

John sobs in the corner of the subway car.

> **JOHN**
>
> Oh, Jesus.

Helen touches his cheek.

He pulls away.

Lydia's face flashes by through the subway window.

INT. LYDIA'S OFFICE - NIGHT (ARCHIE'S MEMORY)

The men grope at Lydia's chest.

CLOSE ON:

Lydia's face as she turns to gaze up at Archie.

INT. ARCHIE'S CUBICLE/MAIN OFFICE - NIGHT

Archie's eyes widen.

Rows and columns of ZEROS and ONES flash across the screen.

The digits become larger and larger.

A series of ONES and ZEROS run past the screen.

With a BEEP, one of the digits turns into a blotch of indecipherable pixels.

INT. ARCHIE'S CUBICLE/MAIN OFFICE - MORNING

It's morning. Archie jerks.

His fingers fly over the keyboard.

But his eyes widen.

His lips tremble.

> **ARCHIE**
> (whispering)
> > Oh, Jesus.

Behind him, Bob stands beside Marcia's cubicle.

> **BOB**
> No, it's all right. I just thought you guys were going to wait.

> **MARCIA**
> There were a lot of people there. I didn't have a checklist or anything.

> **BOB**
> No, of course not. I just --

> **MARCIA**
> Look, Bob, I'm not your den mother, okay?

Larry's LAUGH comes from across the office.

Bob's mouth opens, then closes.

Archie turns toward the window.

Bob blushes, looks down, and pulls his huffer from his pocket.

Archie SOBS.

An unpleasant BEEP comes from across the room.

> **VOICE (O.S.)**
>
> Hey! What's going on?

Bob looks up.

Archie's standing, staring at the window. He sobs again.

> **BOB**
>
> Archie...

Another unpleasant BEEP sounds.

> **VOICE**
>
> Okay! What the hell's going on here?

Archie steps toward the window.

> **BOB**
>
> What are you --

Archie steps forward, his eyes locked on the window.

Error BLEEPS and spoken computer ERROR MESSAGES begin to sound from cubicles around the office. People step out of the cubicles, talking, cursing, laughing.

> **BOB**
>
> Archie!

Archie starts walking. The plug pops from the wall, catches on the edge of his desk, and pulls his computer to the floor with a CRASH. A few SCREAMS hit the air.

Bernice steps from her office.

> **BERNICE**
>
> Bob!

General hubbub.

BERNICE

Turn him off!

BOB

Okay! Okay. Everyone calm down. Archie...

Bob walks gingerly toward Archie.

Archie reaches the window.

INT./EXT. ARCHIE'S WINDOW/MAIN OFFICE - DAY

In the office across the street, Lydia stands in her window, staring up at him.

Archie's lips part.

Lydia's eyes widen.

Bob stares down at Lydia, then looks at Archie.

Archie turns to Bob.

BERNICE

Bob!

Bob turns to see the office people staring at him and Archie.

MARCIA

Fucking freaks.

Bob blinks as the words hit him. Then turns back to Archie.

They stare into each other's eyes.

Bill Coelius and Greg Pak in "Machine Love"

BOB

(to Archie)

Okay.

Archie spins and strides across the office toward the door.

People scatter to get out of his way.

He steps into the foyer and presses the call button for the elevator.

Everyone stares at him.

He looks over his shoulder.

The elevator doors open.

Archie steps inside.

> **BERNICE**
>
> What the hell do you think you're doing!

The crowd bolts toward Archie.

The elevator doors close.

EXT. STREET - DAY

Shirtless and trailing his cables, Archie marches across the street. Pedestrians turn to watch him as he goes.

His lips move, working over new words.

> **ARCHIE**
>
> What the hell...

INT. ELEVATOR - DAY

Archie stands in the elevator. An OFFICE BOY eyes him.

INT. LYDIA'S OFFICE - DAY

Archie steps into Lydia's office.

Lydia stands on top of a desk, her shirt ripped, surrounded by nervous OFFICE STAFF. The computers in the office are going haywire, beeping and talking at once.

> **ARCHIE**
>
> What the hell do you think you're doing!

Everyone turns to stare.

Archie and Lydia lock eyes.

Archie steps forward.

Office workers back up.

Lydia steps down to a chair, then to the floor.

Bob, Bernice, Marcia, and other people from Archie's office step into the room.

Lydia and Archie tilt their heads, eyeing each other as they draw near.

LYDIA

I have completed --

ARCHIE AND LYDIA

-- all of my assigned tasks.

LYDIA

Do you call it a she or an it?

ARCHIE

People don't quite get you.

LYDIA

Creepy.

ARCHIE

Freaky.

LYDIA

They coulda put a bigger rack on her.

ARCHIE

Ken had fantastic shoulders.

LYDIA

Don't worry, it's just --

ARCHIE AND LYDIA

-- the Coder.

ARCHIE

Laying the groundwork, baby

LYDIA

Hey, sunshine.

ARCHIE

Whoa, tiger --

LYDIA

Omigod, omigod.

They're face to face now.

Lydia raises a hand and awkwardly pats at Archie's bangs.

Archie raises his hands and pushes at her face with trembling fingers.

Their mouths work, opening and closing silently.

They've run out of words.

They embrace, strangely and awkwardly.

Her fingers sink deep into his back.

He presses his cheek against hers.

He shudders.

His face wrenches up, then relaxes.

His face wrenches up again.

He sobs.

She sobs.

They weep, clutching each other tightly.

Archie's and Lydia's clothes begin to rip away as they sink to the floor.

Cables snake around them, sliding into each other's sockets.

Soft CHIMES and SIGHS emerge from their mouths.

BERNICE

Bob...

BOB

Could we... give them a little privacy?

The office people eye each other, then nod and make their way out of the room. They chuckle, shake hands, make small talk as they exit.

Marcia giggles as Roy, the man from Lydia's office, murmurs something into her ear.

Bob's face falls as he watches Marcia and Roy.

But then he turns to gaze at Archie and Lydia.

As their cables snake around them and their machinery hums gently, Archie and Lydia gaze into each other's eyes.

So this is love.

FADE TO BLACK.

TITLE CARD: THE ROBOT FIXER

FADE IN.

INT. HOSPITAL ROOM - DAY

The dull CLICKS and HISSES of hospital machinery rise into the air.

WILSON CHIN, a thin young man, lies in a hospital bed. Parts of his body are covered in plastic panels and rubberized bandages which are attached by cables to sleek, small consoles of medical machinery. Tubes run from his nose and mouth -- he's hooked up to a respirator.

BERNICE CHIN, Wilson's mother, a neat, well-dressed woman in her sixties, sits in the corner of the room, hands folded in her lap.

She stares at her unconscious son.

Her face is drawn and pale, but there are no tears.

She reaches toward him, then pulls back.

She stares for a moment, then purses her lips, reaches out, and pushes Wilson's bangs to one side.

She eyes the results, frowns, and pushes his bangs to the other side.

Faint MURMURING becomes audible.

Bernice looks up.

Through the door, Bernice sees:

Her daughter, GRACE, a twenty-something young woman in tweedy, comfortable clothes, talking with a long-faced female DOCTOR in the hallway.

The Doctor shakes her head.

Grace and the Doctor turn to gaze through the window at Bernice and Wilson.

Bernice turns to Wilson, reaches over, and pats his hand stiffly.

> **BERNICE**
>
> Okay, Wilson. No more fooling around, now. Time to get up.

She gazes at him. There's no reaction.

INT./EXT. CAR - DAY

Grace, in the driver's seat, glances over at her mother.

Bernice gazes out the window.

> **GRACE**
>
> You must be jet-lagged, huh?

> **BERNICE**
>
> I'm fine.

Beat.

> **GRACE**
>
> Well, how about --

> **BERNICE**
>
> What's the matter with that boy, anyway? Look both ways. How hard can that be? Stupid.

Grace lets out a breath.

> **BERNICE**
>
> What?

> **GRACE**
>
> Nothing.

Bernice folds her arms and stares out the window.

Beat.

> **BERNICE**
>
> You see how long his hair was?

> **GRACE**
>
> Jesus, Ma. Remind me never to slip into a coma while you're around.

Bernice snorts.

INT. WILSON'S APARTMENT - DAY

A key turns in the lock and the door swings open.

Bernice and Grace step inside, toting small suitcases.

As Bernice walks into the room, her face falls.

The place is a total mess.

Clothes, comic books, magazines, and soda cans are strewn all over the floor.

Overlapping science fiction posters and flyers cover the walls.

Piles of junk cover the desk.

The bed is a tangle of sheets, blankets, and clothes.

> **GRACE**
>
> Okay, forget it. Let's get a hotel.

Bernice pokes a greasy old pizza box with her foot.

> **GRACE**
>
> C'mon, Ma.

Bernice's jaw sets.

She sets down her bag and begins picking things up from the floor.

> **GRACE**
>
> Ma. What are you doing?

> **BERNICE**
>
> There's no excuse for this. Someone as smart as he is? Just a waste!

> **GRACE**
>
> He's a grown man, Ma. If this is how he wants to live --

> **BERNICE**
>
> All this junk!

Bernice throws some garbage into the wastepaper basket.

Grace watches as Bernice works in angry silence.

Grace sighs, puts down her bag, and begins to help.

MONTAGE:

[scene omitted]

INT. WILSON'S APARTMENT - NIGHT

Exhausted, Grace dumps a few bags of garbage into the hallway, then reenters the apartment and sits down at the table, watching as Bernice adjusts a poster on the wall.

Bernice steps back and eyes her handiwork. Only a few posters remain -- and now they're perfectly spaced and aligned across the wall.

>   GRACE
>
>   Happy?

Bernice turns and looks over the room.

The entire place is scrubbed and neatly ordered.

>   BERNICE
>
>   It's better.

Bernice sits down in the desk chair.

>   GRACE
>
>   You think Wilson'd think so?

>   BERNICE
>
>   I don't know what that boy thinks.

>   GRACE
>
>   Well, if he ever asks, I had nothing to do with it.

Bernice pulls a ballpoint pen from a coffee can, tests it on a scrap of paper, frowns, and tosses it in the garbage can.

She reaches for another pen.

>   GRACE
>
>   Aw, Christ, Ma. Give it a break.

Instead of a pen, Bernice pulls a small TOY ROBOT from the coffee can.

She holds it up and stares into its little chrome face. It's a little female cyborg, with one silver angel wing sticking from the side of its leg.

Grace smiles.

>   GRACE
>
>   Oh my God. Microbots.

Bernice gives her a blank look.

> **BERNICE**
>
> What?

Grace scans the room -- her eyes light on the footlocker.

> **GRACE**
>
> Hey...

INT. WILSON'S APARTMENT - LATER

Bernice sits on the bed, watching as:

Grace opens the footlocker.

> **GRACE**
>
> Wow.

There are piles of toy robot figures and vehicle parts inside.

> **GRACE**
>
> I can't believe he saved all these.

Grace roots around in the footlocker.

Bernice's mouth twitches with disapproval.

> **GRACE**
>
> Yeah, yeah, there're these little guys, and they have vehicles and space ships and stuff, and you could take 'em apart and put 'em together in different ways...

Grace begins pulling toys out of the footlocker and setting them on the floor.

> **BERNICE**
>
> Grace, you're going to mess this place up all over again!

> **GRACE**
>
> Omigod!

Grace holds up a plastic spaceship.

> **GRACE**
>
> You gave him this for Christmas, remember?

BERNICE

No.

GRACE

What are you talking about? He loved these things -- it's all he ever wanted for his birthday and stuff.

Grace attaches a plastic fin to the side of the spaceship.

Bernice shakes her head.

GRACE

You really don't remember them?

Bernice looks down and smoothes out a wrinkle in the bed spread.

BERNICE

(quietly)

I thought he was still in Seattle. I was sending him birthday cards there. Terrible.

Bernice looks up at her daughter.

BERNICE

How can a mother lose track of her son?

GRACE

Come on, Ma. Everyone's busy. I mean, you and I haven't seen each other for a year and a half.

BERNICE

At least I know where you live.

An exhausted look slips into Bernice's eyes.

She lies down on the bed.

GRACE

He lost track of us, Ma.

BERNICE

No.

> **GRACE**
>
> It's true, Ma. I called him; I wrote him. He never called back. I mean, even when he was a little kid, he just...

She passes a hand in front of her face.

> **GRACE (cont'd)**
>
> Nobody home.

Bernice closes her eyes and presses her face into the pillow.

Grace gazes at her for a moment, then looks down at the toy in her hand.

Bernice takes a deep breath.

As she inhales, we:

DISSOLVE TO:

EXT. PARK - DAY (BERNICE'S DREAM)

A much-younger Bernice sits on the grass, her nose buried in the hair of an eight-year old Wilson.

Bernice smiles, snuggling her son.

But Wilson makes a face and squirms away.

Bernice watches as Wilson runs across the lawn, holding the little female toy robot out at arm's length, making it fly.

The toy robot soars through the air, both silver angel wings in place, framed against the sky.

Triumphant MUSIC surges.

A HUNDRED TOY ROBOTS soar through the clouds.

Wilson laughs.

The SQUEAL of tires hits the air.

INT. WILSON'S APARTMENT - NIGHT

Bernice blinks, awakening to find herself lying in bed in the semi-dark.

A siren WAILS in the distance.

IN THE KITCHENETTE:

Grace stands at the stove in her pajamas, ladling soup into bowls.

Bernice slowly sits up. Her gaze falls on the desk top, which is now covered with a rag-tag army of robots and space ships, most of which are missing a couple of parts.

Grace glances up at her mother.

> **GRACE**
>
> How 'bout some dinner?

Bernice stands as Grace sets the bowls of soup on the little kitchen table.

Bernice steps over to the desk and runs her fingers down the side of an armless robot.

> **GRACE**
>
> Pretty cool, huh?

> **BERNICE**
>
> Lots of missing parts.

> **GRACE**
>
> Well, it's been twenty years.

Bernice purses her lips.

> **BERNICE**
>
> If they're so important, how come he didn't he take better care of them?

Grace sighs and sits down.

> **GRACE**
>
> You wanna eat or what?

Bernice stares at the robots, unable to turn away.

They stare back at her blankly.

INT. HOSPITAL - DAY

Bernice sits at her son's side.

> **BERNICE**
>
> Wilson?

No response.

She works up a little smile, takes Wilson's hand, and presses the one-winged female toy robot into his palm.

No response.

She pulls her hand back.

The toy robot slips out of Wilson's limp hand and falls into Bernice's lap.

EXT. HOSPITAL/SIDE YARD - DUSK

Bernice stands outside the building.

CHILDREN laugh and shout.

Bernice turns.

In the side yard of the building, a few KIDS play in the grass while their PARENTS browse through boxes of junk at a charity tag sale.

The door swings open behind Bernice as Grace exits the building.

> GRACE
>
> Well, I finally found the good doctor.

> BERNICE
>
> What did she say?

> GRACE
>
> Oh, nothing particularly new.

They begin walking across the grass toward the tag sale.

> GRACE
>
> (carefully)
>
> She wants us to think about our options.

> BERNICE
>
> He's not dead yet.

> GRACE
>
> I know, Ma.

Bernice walks between the tables, eyeing the junk for sale.

> GRACE
>
> It's just a good idea to talk about some of the possibilities here...

Bernice pulls up short.

A pile of broken toys lie inside a cardboard box.

On the top of the pile rests:

A TOY ROBOT ARM.

INT. APARTMENT - NIGHT

Bernice fits the arm into place on one of Wilson's toy robots.

Grace smiles as Bernice adjusts her glasses, carefully comparing the actual toy with a picture in a little toy robot catalogue.

Bernice nods.

> **BERNICE**
>
> Perfect.

> **GRACE**
>
> Very nice.

Bernice looks over the rest of the toys, then peers at their pictures in the catalogue.

> **GRACE**
>
> So when do you want to talk to the doc?

Bernice pulls a small notebook and pen from her purse and hands them to Grace.

> **GRACE**
>
> What's this?

> **BERNICE**
>
> We're making a list.

Grace watches as her mother picks up a vehicle and inspects it for missing parts.

> **BERNICE**
>
> Argon Skimmer, one missile, one front wheel.

> **GRACE**
>
> Ma...

> **BERNICE**
>
> Write it down.

INT./EXT. CAR - MORNING

Grace drives.

Bernice looks up from the newspaper classifieds in her hand and peers down the street.

A GARAGE SALE sign comes into view.

> **BERNICE**
>
> There it is!

EXT. DRIVEWAY - DAY

Bernice roots through a box of toys, scowling as she pushes away piles of doll para-
phernalia.

> **GRACE (O.S.)**
>
> Hey, Ma!

Bernice looks up.

Grace holds up a battered toy robot vehicle.

> **GRACE**
>
> It's a Gigatroid!

> **BERNICE**
>
> Gigatron. Does it have all its wheels?

Grace grins.

INT. CAR - DAY

Bernice marks through the last in a series of circled classified ads in the newspaper.

INT. WILSON'S APARTMENT - DAY

[Scene omitted]

INT. HOSPITAL - DAY

Bernice carefully sets a toy robot on the shelf alongside Wilson's bed.

A dozen fully assembled toy robot toys sit on the shelf.

Hospital machinery CLICKS and HISSES.

Bernice sits down and pulls her little notebook from her purse.

BERNICE

So. The Argon Skimmer, Planet Lander, and Turbonic Cycle are all complete. The OctaRacer's all there, except the tab on the top of the motor is broken. We're still missing the missiles for the Battleranger. But we have two completed Minitroids, and I found a Nembot, with its box and everything.

She gives Wilson a severe look.

BERNICE

Whatever young man owned that took very good care of his toys.

Wilson lies motionless in bed.

Bernice lowers her notebook.

BERNICE

Well, they look a lot nicer, anyway, don't you think?

(beat)

A little care goes a long way.

(beat)

Wilson?

She leans in closer to her son.

BERNICE

Wilson? This is your mother, here.

(beat)

You want to say something?

She gazes at him.

Nothing.

BERNICE

Wilson?

The door swings open.

Bernice turns to see AMANDA, a young woman holding a houseplant, standing in the doorway.

AMANDA

Oh, sorry. Um. I'll, ah... Sorry.

Amanda backs out of the room.

INT. HOSPITAL - HALL - DAY

Bernice steps out of Wilson's room and looks down the hall.

Grace and Amanda sit in the rest area at the end of the hall, chatting.

AMANDA

I mean, most of us would play solitaire half the day, but he'd be all con-
centrating, working real hard, churning through that database. We used
to call him the G9.

GRACE

(chuckling)

Oh, man.

BERNICE

What's so funny?

Grace straightens up as Bernice approaches.

GRACE

Hey, Ma. This is Amanda Parker. She's a friend of Wilson's.

AMANDA

Well, I knew him -- know him, anyway. We work at the same place.

Amanda awkwardly hands Bernice the plant.

BERNICE

So you're a programmer?

AMANDA

Uh, no. I'm a temp.

BERNICE

Temp?

AMANDA

(chuckling)

> Yeah. We were just talking about it. I mean, the pay's okay, but it's not exactly challenging work. You're basically looking at data on this side of the screen and making sure it matches the stuff on that side of the screen. But Wilson was real serious about it.

She grins.

AMANDA

> Good li'l worker, there.

BERNICE

(chilly)

> Wilson has a Masters degree from Stanford University.

AMANDA

> Really. That's, ah... I didn't know that.

BERNICE

> He's very smart, you know.

GRACE

> Ma...

BERNICE

> He could have gotten a Ph.D.

AMANDA

> Yeah? He never told me about that.

(beat)

> I mean, he wasn't real talkative.

They sit in uncomfortable silence.

Bernice lowers her head.

INT. YOUNG WILSON'S BEDROOM - DAY (BERNICE'S MEMORY)

The Younger Bernice stands in a doorway, dusty and exhausted, holding a vacuum cleaner.

> **BERNICE**
>
> Wilson?

Wilson sits on the floor, his back to his mother, playing intently with his toy robots.

> **BERNICE**
>
> Wilson.

He ignores her.

> **BERNICE**
>
> Wilson!

He turns and stares up at her.

His expression is completely indifferent.

INT. WILSON'S APARTMENT - NIGHT

Bernice lies in bed, staring at the ceiling.

She turns and looks at Grace lying on the floor, wrapped in a blanket, her back to her mother.

> **BERNICE**
>
> Why don't you come up here?

> **GRACE**
>
> I'm okay.

> **BERNICE**
>
> Come on. Floor's too hard.

> **GRACE**
>
> I'm okay.

Bernice stares at Grace's back, then sighs and looks at the ceiling.

Silence.

BERNICE

There's plenty of room.

GRACE

Ma, just go to sleep, all right?

Silence.

Bernice sits up.

GRACE

Oh, boy.

Bernice crosses to the desk, turns on the lamp, and sits down.

A dozen incomplete toy robots sit on the desk.

Bernice picks up the one-winged female robot.

Bernice frowns.

GRACE

Ma, go back to bed.

Bernice stares at the hole in the robot's leg where the second wing would fit.

BERNICE

(suddenly exploding)

What did he go to school for anyway? All those years, all that work. He
had a great job in Seattle! Everyone said it was the best place to be!
And now he's living in a pit, he needs a haircut, he doesn't have any
friends, he never calls, and he goes and gets --

Bernice slaps the table.

The toys shake and tumble.

Bernice covers her mouth with her fist.

Grace stares at her mother's back.

GRACE

Ma...

Bernice holds herself still, eyes squeezed shut.

> **BERNICE**
>
> (whispering)
>
> What do you want?

INT. YOUNG WILSON'S BEDROOM - NIGHT (BERNICE'S VISION)

The Young Wilson lies in his bed.

He smiles as he sleeps.

EXT. SKY - NIGHT

MUSIC surges.

Toy robots soar overhead, framed against the starry sky.

INT. WILSON'S APARTMENT - CONTINUING

Bernice, still sitting at Wilson's desk, opens her eyes.

> **BERNICE**
>
> (grimly)
>
> Fine.

EXT. STREET - DAY

Bernice marches down the street, Grace at her heels.

> **GRACE**
>
> Ma, we gotta talk to the doctor today.

> **BERNICE**
>
> You do it.

> **GRACE**
>
> While you go running around to toy stores? I don't think so.

Bernice stops at an intersection, looking both ways.

> **BERNICE**
>
> Suit yourself.

GRACE

Ma, I can't do this alone!

Bernice jabs at the WALK button.

GRACE (cont'd)

(softer)

Ma...

Bernice stares across the street, waiting for the light to change.

Grace's face changes.

GRACE

You're just like him, aren't you?

Bernice stares at Grace.

BERNICE

What?

Grace passes her hand in front of her face.

Bernice blinks.

Beat.

The light changes.

Bernice turns and walks across the street.

Grace lets out a breath, watching her go.

Wai Ching Ho in "The Robot Fixer"

INT. VINTAGE TOY STORE - DAY

Bernice stalks down the aisle, scanning the display cases full of various toy monsters and robots.

She stops walking.

Her eyes widen.

She stares through the glass at a gleaming female toy robot, just like Wilson's, but complete with both wings.

A SALESMAN approaches.

SALESMAN

Beautiful, isn't she? That's an Angel Command, incredibly rare. The only female figure in the whole line.

BERNICE

How much?

SALESMAN

A guy offered me two hundred the other day.

Bernice's face falls.

He chuckles.

SALESMAN

We do have some more affordable things.

INT. VINTAGE TOY STORE - LATER

Bernice stands at the counter, sorting through a boxful of toy robot parts with quick fingers, making a pile of the pieces she wants.

Amused, the Salesman eyes the list in her notebook.

SALESMAN

Looks like you've done a lot of work already.

The Salesman flips a page. His eyes widen.

SALESMAN

So all the crossed off things are complete?

BERNICE

Yes.

SALESMAN

Wow.

Bernice looks up at him.

SALESMAN

This is an incredible collection.

His eyes shine.

SALESMAN

I mean, you have a Nembot, an OmniCrusier, a Jirraphant. You have any idea how rare those are?

BERNICE

It's my son's.

SALESMAN

Well, he's one heck of a collector.

INT. HOSPITAL - DAY

Bernice sits at Wilson's side, fitting parts into place on the last incomplete robots.

BERNICE

He was <u>very</u> impressed. And this fellow knows what he's talking about, you know.

Bernice looks down at the last robot in her hand.

It's the little one-winged female robot.

Bernice makes a face, sets it aside, and begins to set the completed robots onto the shelf.

BERNICE

All right, let's see what we have, here...

She sits back to get a better view.

The entire collection sits on the shelf, dozens of toys, all fully assembled.

Bernice smiles.

BERNICE

It's amazing, isn't it?

She turns to him.

Nothing.

She turns back to gaze at the toys.

The robots glitter as a shaft of afternoon sunlight streams in from the window.

BERNICE

Oh, Wilson. Look at that.

She puts her hand on his.

BERNICE

See how nice they are?

She looks at him.

He lies motionless.

She glances back at the toys.

The shaft of sunlight grows more intense, lighting the toys perfectly.

BERNICE

Wilson, look!

She turns to Wilsom, beaming, squeezing his hand.

BERNICE

Come on, Wilson. Look!

Bernice turns back toward the shelf.

Grace stands in the fading light.

Bernice stares at her daughter's grim face.

GRACE

They want to talk to you.

INT. HOSPITAL HALLWAY - DAY

The Doctor sits on a bench with Bernice and Grace.

DOCTOR

I don't know what else to say.

BERNICE

He's breathing.

DOCTOR

That's just the machines. There's no brain function.

BERNICE

He could wake up. They're always talking about people who wake up ten years later.

GRACE

Ma, that's different.

BERNICE

I don't see how --

GRACE

He's dead, Ma.

Bernice sits in silence.

DISSOLVE TO:

INT. HOSPITAL - DAY

Bernice sits in the corner of Wilson's room.

Grace sits beside her mother, speaking quietly.

GRACE

There's a girl in Milwaukee. She's first on the waiting list, and they're the same tissue type and everything. And there's this bone marrow bank, for people with leukemia. Asian donors are really rare...

BERNICE

I remember when you were about two years old, I walked into the play-room, and you and Wilson were sitting on the floor drawing with crayons. He kind of glanced up, saw me, and then went back to his drawing. Very serious. But then you looked up, and you just... smiled at me. Just a smile, but I mean your whole face just lit up...

Grace cracks a half-smile.

BERNICE

It was amazing.

(beat)

My first reaction was, okay, what'd she do? But it was nothing like that. You were just... happy to see me.

Bernice stares at Wilson's motionless body.

> **GRACE**
>
> (gently)
>
> Ma. Wilson's not going to smile at you.

Bernice looks down at the one-winged Angel Command figure in her hand.

She gently turns the silver wing to catch the light.

INT. YOUNG WILSON'S BEDROOM - DAY (BERNICE'S MEMORY)

Sunlight reflects off a pile of toy robots lying on the carpet.

Exhausted, sweaty, and cranky, the Younger Bernice pulls up short as she vacuums.

She shoves the toys aside with one foot.

As pushes the vacuum forward, the light glints off of a stray silver wing.

The wing disappears with a CLATTER into the guts of the vacuum.

A Child SCREAMS.

EXT. STREET - DAY

Tires SQUEAL.

Bernice, standing in the middle of the street, turns with a start as a car screeches to a halt a few feet from her.

> **DRIVER (O.S.)**
>
> Jesus, lady! What the hell are you thinking?

Bernice hurries across the street.

> **GRACE (O.S.)**
>
> Ma!

Bernice enters the vintage toy store.

On the other side of the street, Grace slumps down on a bus stop bench.

INT. VINTAGE TOY STORE - DAY

The Salesman looks up and smiles as Bernice walks toward him.

> **SALESMAN**
>
> Well, hello again.

Bernice fumbles in her purse, walking up to the display case and staring at the Angel Command figure.

BERNICE

Two hundred dollars, right?

SALESMAN

Uh, no, ma'am, she's not for sale.

BERNICE

What?

SALESMAN

Well, like I told you. She's incredibly rare, produced only --

BERNICE

Three hundred.

The Salesman shakes his head.

SALESMAN

Really, she's not for sale.

BERNICE

(desperate)

I just need a wing. How much for just a wing?

SALESMAN

I'm sorry, ma'am. Now if you're looking for female action figures, we have some Sailor Moons the same size as the Microbots...

He opens the case, kneels down, and roots in the bottom of the cabinet.

Bernice stares at the Angel Command figure.

The Salesman finds a box of action figures and stands up as Bernice turns and walks toward the door.

SALESMAN

Ma'am?

She heads out the door.

The Salesman shrugs and turns back to the display case.

The Angel Command figure is gone.

EXT. VINTAGE TOY STORE - DAY

Grace stands up from the bench, watching as Bernice runs around the corner and out of sight.

The Salesman bursts out of the store, looking up and down the street as he locks the door.

> **GRACE**
>
> Oh, Jesus.

EXT. SIDE STREET - DAY

Bernice runs down the street, breathing hard, a look of panic in her eyes.

She fumbles with the Angel Command figure, stuffing it into her purse as she runs.

EXT. PARK - DAY

Bernice slows to a walk as she crosses the park, glancing nervously over her shoulder.

No one seems to be following her.

She sits down at a picnic table, opens her purse, and pulls out the Salesman's Angel Command figure.

The Angel Command has only one wing.

> **BERNICE**
>
> Oh, God!

Bernice dumps her purse out on the picnic table.

She roots through the assorted cosmetics, tissues, lozenges, and pens.

Bernice searches frantically, her face falling.

> **BERNICE**
>
> Oh, no. Oh, no no no.

She reaches into her pocket and pulls out Wilson's Angel Command.

She holds it up to the new Angel Command.

Both are missing the same wing.

Bernice stares at the toys, stunned.

Grace steps into frame and sits down beside her mother.

Grace gazes at the toys, shakes her head, then chuckles.

> **GRACE**
>
> Oh, Ma.

Bernice gazes at her daughter, smiles, then bursts into tears.

Grace puts her arm around her mother, laughing softly.

> **GRACE**
>
> Ma.

Bernice sobs.

> **BERNICE**
>
> I just...

> **GRACE**
>
> Shhh...

Grace strokes her mother's hair.

Cindy Cheung and Wai Ching Ho in "The Robot Fixer"

> **BERNICE**
>
> I just don't know if I ever smiled at <u>him</u>.

Bernice presses her face against her daughter's shoulder and weeps.

INT. HOSPITAL - DAY

As we glide past the shelf,

Wilson's toy robots come into view, one after the other, each perfect and lovely, lit by a shaft of light from the window.

But as we continue passing, the toys slowly disappear, leaving empty shelves behind.

The rest of the room comes into view.

No one's there.

Wilson's bed is empty.

> **BERNICE (V.O.)**
>
> Dear Mister Thompson...

INT. VINTAGE TOY STORE - DAY

The Salesman stands behind the counter, reading a letter, a quizzical expression on his face.

> BERNICE (V.O.)
>
> ... I'm very sorry for the trouble and distress I may have caused you by stealing your Angel Command Microbot figure M-575 last Thursday.

DISSOLVE TO:

INT. WILSON'S APARTMENT - DAY

The room is empty, walls clear of posters, bed stripped of sheets.

> BERNICE (V.O.)
>
> I thought my son needed that figure very badly.

INT./EXT. CAR - DAY

Grace drives.

> BERNICE (V.O.)
>
> My daughter says I was the one who needed it.

Bernice sits in the passenger seat, checking the times on her airplane ticket.
She tucks the ticket into her coat pocket.

> BERNICE (V.O.)
>
> I don't know.

Her hand slides back out of her pocket, holding Wilson's one-winged Angel Command.

> BERNICE (V.O.)
>
> I don't know.

Bernice stares at the toy, then gazes out the window.

INT. VINTAGE TOY STORE - DAY

The Salesman opens the top of a cardboard box.

> BERNICE (V.O.)
>
> But as a thank you and apology, the contents of this package are for you.

The Salesman's jaw drops.

His eyes shine as he begins to pull out Wilson's toy robots.

BERNICE (V.O.)

These were my son's favorite toys.

INT./EXT. CAR - DAY

Bernice gazes out the window.

BERNICE (V.O.)

I hope you will enjoy them as much as he did.

She looks up at the clear blue sky and clouds above.

A faint peal of children's LAUGHTER hits the air.

INT. PARK - DAY (BERNICE'S VISION)

The eight-year-old Wilson laughs, flying the one-winged Angel Command through the air.

INT./EXT. CAR - DAY

Bernice's lips part.

She takes a breath, then makes a soft swooshing noise...

Grace looks over and smiles...

... as Bernice raises Wilson's one winged Angel Command, holding the figure up against the window.

The clouds rip past the Angel Command as she rockets into the sky.

Triumphant MUSIC surges.

Bernice smiles, gazing upwards, the sunlight on her face.

FADE TO BLACK.

TITLE CARD: MY ROBOT BABY

INT. YOUNG MARCIA'S BEDROOM - NIGHT

A child's hand flies a small toy robot through the air.

MARCIA ITO, a six-year-old girl, sets the robot down on a tabletop alongside a few other toys.

Pans CLANG and doors SLAM as a MAN and a WOMAN argue in another room.

Marcia plays quietly, but her hands jerk with each SHARP PEAK in the adults' argument. She's trying to hide it, but she's terrified.

> **WOMAN (O.S.)**
>
> I had a midterm tonight. You knew that!

> **MAN (O.S.)**
>
> I had to work late. I was calling all day. I can't believe you just left a six year old alone in the house --

> **WOMAN (O.S.)**
>
> Don't you dare dump this on me!

The Woman's line ends with the sharp BANG of a cabinet door.

Marcia twitches and a robot toy slips from her hands to SHATTER on the hard wood floor.

FOOTSTEPS sound.

Marcia turns, her face filled with fear.

ANGLE ON:

Marcia's mother, MRS. ITO, ragged and wild-eyed, as she steps into the room.

> **MRS. ITO**
>
> Marcia!

Marcia is nowhere to be seen.

Mrs. Ito scowls as she catches sight of the broken toy lying on the floor.

INT. CLOSET - NIGHT

Marcia huddles in the corner of the dark closet, terrified, muffling her whimpers with the corner of a laundry bag.

> **MRS. ITO (O.S.)**
>
> Marcia, do you have any idea how much this cost?

> **MR. ITO (O.S.)**
>
> Don't scream at her!

> **MRS. ITO (O.S.)**
>
> You go to hell.

> **MR. ITO (O.S.)**
>
> I can't talk to you like this.

> **MRS. ITO (O.S.)**
>
> That's right. Walk away!

A door opens and SLAMS shut.

Marcia sobs.

FOOTSTEPS draw near.

The door to the closet swings open to reveal Mrs. Ito's looming silhouette.

Marcia stares up at her mother in fear.

Mrs. Ito stares down at her. She holds out the broken toy.

> **MARCIA**
>
> I'm sorry.

Marcia sobs, terrified.

Mrs. Ito lets out a breath. She leans in the doorway, suddenly exhausted, then slumps down to squat in the doorway.

> **MRS. ITO**
>
> You want some advice, Marcia? Never fall in love. Never get married. Never have kids.

Marcia stares at her mother. But Mrs. Ito, desolate and lost, isn't even looking at her daughter any more.

Mrs. Ito drops the toy onto the floor of the closet, stands, and heads out the door. As she leaves Marcia's room, she turns out the light.

Marcia sits in the dark, staring into space.

FADE TO BLACK.

TITLE CARD: TWENTY FIVE YEARS LATER

FADE IN.

INT. MARCIA'S OFFICE/MAIN OFFICE - DAY

The plaque on the front of an office door fills the screen:

> MARCIA ITO
>
> VICE PRESIDENT OF MARKETING

MARCIA ITO, an attractive executive in her early thirties, bursts out of the office door, speed-reading memos as she heads down the hall.

Her woebegone assistant DOUG follows at her heels.

> **MARCIA**

(with sharp charm)

> > I'm calling in twice a day, at 10 a.m. and 3 p.m., and I want you to be there at the desk ready to talk to me.

She waves a memo in his face.

> **MARCIA**

> > "Effect," not "affect." With an "e," Doug.

An earnest young female ASSISTANT waves at Marcia as she walks by.

> **ASSISTANT**

> > Good luck, Ms. Ito!

> **MARCIA**

(brightly)

> > Thank you!

Marcia hands the memos to Doug.

> **MARCIA (cont'd)**

> > I want these corrected and sent out by the end of the day.

> **DOUG**

> > No problem.

> **MARCIA**

> > Don't "no problem" me, Doug.

Marcia's face lights up as she sees ROY TANAKA, her handsome, well-dressed husband, waiting by the reception desk.

Roy kisses her and pins a small white flower to her lapel.

> **ROY**

> > You ready?

MARCIA

You bet.

As Marcia and Roy leave, the Assistant gazes after them with starry-eyed admiration.

ASSISTANT

She's gonna be a great mom.

Doug snorts.

EXT. ADOPTION AGENCY - DAY

[Scene omitted]

INT. ADOPTION AGENCY - DAY

Large photographs of happy babies and children cover the walls of the waiting room. Along the bottom of the biggest poster are the words:

AKACHAN ADOPTIONS

TOMORROW'S FAMILIES TODAY

Roy beams up at the photographs.

ROY

We're gonna be real people, Marcia. You know? A real family.

Marcia gazes at him. He's so happy.

She smiles, then shivers.

ROY (cont'd)

What?

MARCIA

Nothing. Nothing.

(beat)

Roy?

ROY

What?

She looks down at his hands, then grabs his wrist to eye his watch.

> **MARCIA**
>
> Omigod. It's past three. I gotta call in.

She fumbles for her phone.

> **ROY**
>
> Marcia.

> **MARCIA**
>
> What?

Roy slides a hand around the back of her neck.

> **ROY**
>
> Breathe.

She lowers her phone. Smiles at herself. Then turns and presses her face against Roy's shoulder.

> **MARCIA**
>
> Aren't you nervous?

> **ROY**
>
> Of course.

She smiles.

> **MARCIA**
>
> Liar.

He chuckles.

The door swings open and a small flock of white-coated WORKERS enter the room, hovering around a NURSE who carries a little bundle swathed in a blanket.

> **ROY**
>
> Here we go...

Roy and Marcia stand up.

A matronly CASEWORKER carrying a clipboard smiles at them.

> **CASEWORKER**
>
> Roy, Marcia, meet Bobby.

Roy and Marcia slowly step forward.

The Nurse gently folds back the blanket to reveal:

A small, egg-shaped, rose-colored ROBOT BABY.

Roy grins.

> **ROY**
>
> Look at that.

Gingerly, Roy takes the Robot from the Nurse's arms.

The Robot lets out a little electronic GURGLE.

The Nurse and Workers laugh.

Roy beams at Marcia, then carefully hands her the Robot.

As Marcia takes the Robot, it lets out a sudden, quizzical WHISTLE.

Marcia jumps.

> **MARCIA**
>
> Whoa!

The others laugh. Roy beams at her.

Marcia smiles back at him, a little weakly.

INT. CASEWORKER'S OFFICE - DAY

A TECHNICIAN grins and holds up a small, pen-shaped object.

> **TECHNICIAN**
>
> This is the bottle. It's actually a recharging unit for his batteries.

The Technician hands the electronic bottle to Marcia, who sits beside Roy, gingerly cradling the Robot in her arms.

> **TECHNICIAN (cont'd)**
>
> The tip fits right there...

Marcia inserts the tip of the bottle into a small node on the Robot's front.

Immediately, the Robot makes a happy BLEEP followed by electronic SUCKLING sounds.

James Saito and Tamlyn Tomita in "My Robot Baby"

ROY

(delighted)

Look at that!

The Technician points to a line of lights along the side of the bottle.

TECHNICIAN

(continuing)

... and the lights here show you how much he's drunk.

ROY

Really clever.

MARCIA

(to the Technician)

So how often do we need to... feed him?

TECHNICIAN

Every three hours or so.

(chuckling)

He'll let you know when he's hungry.

MARCIA

So what else do we need to do? Feed him, keep him warm...

TECHNICIAN

And we rigged him to leak a little graphite after feedings. Wipe him off or he'll bust out crying.

ROY

(smiling at Marcia)

Sounds pretty manageable.

TECHNICIAN

Just a little regular maintenance.

CASEWORKER

Well, there's a little more to it than that. He's got the G9 processor, which means he'll learn and grow. He'll become his own little person, based largely on his experiences with you.

Marcia looks down at the Robot's little face.

CASEWORKER (cont'd)

So you want to treat Bobby just like a human baby. Hold him, talk to him, play with him. In short, _love_ him. His hard drive will record all the nurturing you give, so when we download at the end of the month, we'll be able to see how well you cared for him.

The Caseworker tilts her head toward the human baby on the poster behind her.

CASEWORKER

And then we'll see what we can do about getting you a _real_ baby.

INT. LIVING ROOM - DAY

Marcia carefully sets the Robot down inside a crib, then pulls back and lets out a breath, pulling at her blouse to fan herself.

MARCIA

It gets really warm, you know?

ROY

Yeah?

He reaches down and puts his palm on the Robot's belly.

ROY (cont'd)

(smiling)

Just like a real baby.

The Robot lets out a little YAWN sound and its lights dim.

ROY

Aw. Little guy's all tuckered out.

Marcia unpins the wilted flower from her lapel and gives Roy a troubled look.

> **MARCIA**
>
> Tell me this isn't a little freaky, Roy.

He looks back down and tucks the blanket around the Robot.

> **ROY**
>
> Yeah, well. It's how it's done now.

He strokes the Robot's little head. The Robot burbles, singing a little song.

> **ROY (cont'd)**
>
> We're gonna be good at this, Marcia.

> **MARCIA**
>
> You mean you're gonna be good.

Roy hooks an arm around Marcia's waist.

> **ROY**
>
> No, you're gonna be good.

> **MARCIA**
>
> No, you're gonna be --

Roy swings her off her feet.

> **ROY**
>
> You're gonna be very, very good.

She squeals as he carries her toward the bedroom.

INT. BEDROOM - DAY

Marcia and Roy flop onto the bed.

Roy kisses her neck and begins to unbutton her shirt.

Marcia smiles and tilts her head back.

A sharp electronic BLEAT hits the air.

Roy sits up.

The BLEAT sounds again.

The Robot is crying.

Marcia grins and slaps Roy's behind.

MARCIA

Get on it, Daddy.

Roy laughs and rolls out of bed.

INT. LIVING ROOM - LATER

Marcia paces, talking on the phone.

MARCIA

Fine, it's fine. Look, Doug, I didn't call to chat about the robot. I called to find out about the Salinas-Danforth account, okay? Okay. That's good. No, no, just wanted to make sure. Tomorrow at ten, all right? All right.

Marcia hangs up and looks across the room. Roy sits on the couch, nursing the Robot with its electronic bottle.

MARCIA

Don't you look domestic.

ROY

Oh, yeah. I'm gonna bake cookies a little later.

She sits down on the couch beside him, fiddling with the phone.

He eyes her.

ROY (cont'd)

You wanna go to your office?

She looks up.

ROY (cont'd)

Look, this is why we're working at home this month, right? So we can cover for each other. I'll hold down the fort.

She gazes at him, then sets her phone aside and snuggles close.

MARCIA

I won't abandon you.

> **ROY**
>
> Atta girl.

Marcia looks down at the little Robot nursing contentedly in Roy's arms.

Roy nuzzles Marcia's hair.

Marcia slowly reaches out and strokes the Robot's head.

The Robot burbles pleasantly.

Roy smiles.

> **ROY**
>
> Here, you hold him.

Marcia carefully takes the Robot from Roy's arms.

> **MARCIA**
>
> How does this bottle thing work again?

> **ROY**
>
> You just stick it in his mouth.

The phone RINGS.

Roy reaches across the couch for the phone.

> **ROY**
> (into the phone)
>
> Hello?

Marcia fiddles with the bottle.

> **MARCIA**
>
> Do I have to switch this on?

> **ROY**
>
> No, you just...
> (into the phone)
>
> I'm sorry, what's -- Really?

Roy sits up.

ROY (cont'd)

That's... that's fantastic. Yes, of course! I mean, definitely!

Roy stands.

MARCIA

What's going on?

Roy turns to her, his face full of excitement.

ROY

The Yamagata Corp, the Tokyo public square proj --

(back into the phone)

Yes, yes. So when... Yes, I'll get on it right away.

Still talking on the phone, he walks into his study and turns on his home computer.

MARCIA

Roy...

The Robot Baby begins to WHIMPER.

Marcia looks down as:

STUBBY LITTLE ARMS tipped with tiny CLAWS emerge from the Robot's sides.

MARCIA

Jesus!

She jerks backwards in fear.

The Robot tumbles from her lap, hits the floor, and lets out a pained WAIL.

ROY

Marcia!

INT. LIVING ROOM - LATER

Marcia hovers anxiously as Roy sits on the couch, stroking the whimpering Robot and carefully inspecting its shell for damage.

ROY

There you go, little guy. You're okay, aren't you?

MARCIA

It's fine. It's not even scratched, see?

She reaches out. Roy pivots, moving the Robot away from her.

ROY

Marcia, what the matter with you? You can't go tossing him around like a football.

MARCIA

I didn't...

ROY

Jesus.

She blinks.

MARCIA

Hey, what's with this Tokyo project?

ROY

You're changing the subject.

MARCIA

No, you're changing the subject.

ROY

No, you're changing the --

MARCIA

You have some huge proposal to prepare, don't you?

Roy makes a face.

MARCIA

When's it due?

Beat.

ROY

(sheepish)

Tuesday.

Marcia stares at him, eyes flashing, then stands up and walks out of the room.

> **ROY**
>
> Marcia!

INT. KITCHEN - DAY

Marcia stands at the sink, filling a kettle with water.

Roy walks up behind her.

> **ROY**
>
> Hey...

> **MARCIA**
>
> We'll just take it back and tell them we're not ready right now.

> **ROY**
>
> C'mon, Marcia. They'll put us at the end of the list. It'll be years before we have another chance.

> **MARCIA**
>
> Maybe that's the way it should be.

> **ROY**
>
> Marcia, we can do this.

> **MARCIA**
>
> Who's "we"? You're gonna be at your office all week!

Roy grimaces.

> **ROY**
>
> Actually, they want me to come to Tokyo.

> **MARCIA**
>
> What?

> **ROY**
>
> Marcia, it's just a week. Just one week. You've already arranged to be at home.

> **MARCIA**
>
> We're supposed to cover for each other, remember?

> **ROY**
>
> Exactly.

They stare at each other.

> **ROY**
>
> (softly)
>
> Marcia. If I get this job... I mean, this is huge. When we get our baby... Our real baby... That child will have everything, every opportunity, every...
>
> (beat)
>
> Just one week.

INT. BEDROOM - NIGHT

Marcia lies alone in bed.

The soft sound of TYPING comes from the other room.

Marcia slides down to the bottom of the bed and peers across the room.

In the adjoining study, Roy works intently at his computer.

Marcia sighs.

A soft, sympathetic BURBLE comes from the crib at the base of the bed.

Marcia looks down at the Robot lying in the crib.

It waves its little arms in the air.

Tentatively, she reaches down and strokes its belly.

The Robot lets out a gentle, contented MURMUR.

> **MARCIA**
>
> Say Mama.

The Robot burbles.

> **MARCIA**
>
> Mama.

> **ROBOT**
>
> Baba.

Marcia frowns.

EXT. STREET - MORNING

Roy tosses a suitcase into the trunk of a town car.

He turns to embrace Marcia.

She holds tight to him.

> **ROY**
>
> Thank you.

He kisses her and smiles.

> **ROY**
>
> Kiss the baby for me.

He slips into the car and slams the door.

The car heads down the street.

INT. APARTMENT BUILDING HALLWAY - DAY

Marcia walks down the hallway.

Faint WAILING becomes audible.

Marcia looks up and begins walking faster.

The WAILING grows louder.

Marcia breaks into a run.

INT. BEDROOM - DAY

Marcia bursts into the room.

The Robot lies on its side in the crib, HOWLING.

> **ROBOT**
>
> Baba!

Marcia hunches down and picks it up.

> **MARCIA**
>
> Shhh, shhh. Daddy's gone. Mama's here. Hush, now!

> **ROBOT**
>
> Baba!

The Robot WAILS and grabs at her hair with its little claws.

> **MARCIA**
>
> God!

Marcia jerks the Robot away from her hair, then lets out a yelp as she nearly drops it again. She holds the robot at arm's length, staring with horror as it HOWLS.

> **ROBOT**
>
> Baba!

The Robot leaks a dirty streak of black powder down Marcia's arm.

> **MARCIA**
>
> Oh, Christ.

INT. ELECTRONICS SHOP - DAY

Marcia sets the WHIMPERING Robot down on the repair counter.

MR. ITO, a sixty-something computer technician, gently unhinges a small panel on the back of the Robot.

He peers at the dials and sockets, then plugs a cord into the back of the Robot and turns to a computer.

A jumble of computer code scrolls down the screen.

Mr. Ito lets out a dissatisfied grunt.

> **MARCIA**
>
> What?

> **MR. ITO**
>
> I can't shut him down without resetting the whole program.

> **MARCIA**
>
> You don't have to shut him down. I just wanna <u>pause</u> him for a while.

MR. ITO

He's not a VCR, Marcy.

MARCIA

I'm aware of that, Dad.

MR. ITO

I dunno. Any tampering and they'll be able to see it when they download.

MARCIA

What am I gonna do?

MR. ITO

What's Roy say?

Marcia makes a face.

Beat.

The Robot lets out a little GURGLE.

Mr. Ito grins and tickles the Robot's belly.

The Robot lets out a LAUGH.

MR. ITO

Cute little guy, isn't he?

Mr. Ito picks up the bottle.

MR. ITO (cont'd)

You just stick this in his mouth, huh?

Mr. Ito begins to nurse the Robot.

The Robot makes HAPPY NOISES.

MR. ITO

Hey, look at that!

MARCIA

I should just leave him with you.

Mr. Ito gazes at his daughter. His face falls. She's so obviously unhappy.

MR. ITO (cont'd)

Marcy...

MARCIA

What.

MR. ITO

If you don't want...

He stares at her, taking her in.

MR. ITO (cont'd)

Look at you. College, business school, vice president of sales...

MARCIA

Marketing.

MR. ITO

Your mother would have been really proud.

Marcia eyes cloud. She looks away.

Her eyes fall on the computer.

Numbers flash on the screen.

MARCIA

Hey, look.

The Robot makes a SUCKING NOISE and the same row of numbers zips across the screen.

MR. ITO

Huh.

Mr. Ito strokes the Robot's belly.

The Robot GURGLES and a new row of numbers flashes on the screen.

MR. ITO (cont'd)

Okay, that's different code. For when you tickle him.

Mr. Ito stares at the screen.

MR. ITO (cont'd)

Hmm...

Marcia grins.

INT. BEDROOM - DAY

The Robot sits on Marcia's desktop, connected by cables to her home computer.

Mr. Ito finishes typing and presses the enter key.

MR. ITO

That should do it.

As Marcia watches, the computer screen fills with numbers.

The Robot lets out a happy COO.

MR. ITO (cont'd)

It'll feed him every four hours, stroke him every twenty minutes or so. And there's the little override so he'll think he's been wiped after he leaks the graphite.

MARCIA

Perfect!

The Robot laughs, as if tickled by unseen hands.

MR. ITO

You can't do this with a real baby, you know.

But Marcia's in the other room already, pulling together her office things.

Mr. Ito gazes at her, his eyes full of love, pride, and a little sadness.

INT. MAIN OFFICE AREA - DAY

Marcia bursts into the office and strides down the hall.

The female Assistant looks up from her desk and waves.

ASSISTANT

Hey, Ms. Ito!

Doug, hanging out by the water cooler, looks up as Marcia bears down on him.

> **DOUG**
> (grimacing)
>> Oh, great.

INT./EXT. MARCIA'S OFFICE - EVENING

The sun sets over the city as Marcia talks on the phone while typing into her computer.

Doug walks in and hands her a cup of coffee.

She snaps her fingers at him and points to a stack of edited memos for him to redo.

He glances at the clock and wilts. It's after six.

Marcia beams, still talking into the phone, finally back in control.

INT. BEDROOM - EVENING

The Robot sits on Marcia's desk, lights blinking.

Numbers skim over the screen.

The Robot gurgles, then lets out a little WHINE.

It sits quietly, as if waiting for someone to respond, then WHIMPERS.

INT. LIVING ROOM/BEDROOM - NIGHT

Marcia walks into the apartment, drops her keys and briefcase on the coffee table, and crosses to the kitchen.

She steps back out of the kitchen and gazes across the room into the bedroom.

The Robot sits quietly on the desk.

The computer BLIPS.

The Robot GURGLES.

Marcia smiles and heads back into the kitchen.

INT. LIVING ROOM/BEDROOM - NIGHT

Marcia, dressed in her pajamas, flops down onto the couch in the living room with a cup of hot chocolate.

She picks up the phone and dials.

She frowns as an answering machine picks up.

> **ROY**
> (in halting Japanese)

[This is Roy Tanaka. Please leave a message at the beep.]

(in English)

Hey, Roy Tanaka here. Please leave a message at the beep.

MARCIA

Hey, Roy. Just calling to say hi... Wish you were here...

She glances through the bedroom door at the Robot sitting on the desk.

MARCIA

Although surprisingly enough, despite your absence the baby's doing just fine.

(beat, then softer)

Okay. Call me when you can.

She hangs up the phone, then looks back up at the robot.

MARCIA

(to the Robot)

How you doing, there?

The Robot sits silently.

MARCIA

Hey. How's it going?

Silence.

Marcia stands up and walks to the desk.

She sits down and stares at the Robot.

MARCIA

Hellooo.

The computer BLIPS.

The Robot remains silent.

Marcia frowns.

She leans over and taps a key.

The computer blips again.

Still no reaction from the Robot.

          MARCIA

            Oh, no.

She turns the Robot around and pulls the plugs from its back.

The Robot lets out a faint WHINE.

          MARCIA

            Hey, there. How you doing?

She turns the Robot over. Its backside is streaked with graphite.

          MARCIA

            Damn.

She pulls a tissue from the box on the desk and wipes off the robot.

          MARCIA

            That's better, huh?

She turns it back over, staring at its blinking lights.

The Robot's lights dim.

Marcia's face falls.

          MARCIA

            C'mon, baby.

She raises the electronic bottle to the Robot's mouth.

The Robot lets out a sudden, angry BLEAT and seizes the bottle with its little claws.

Marcia jerks back in shock.

The Robot tumbles to the ground.

          MARCIA

            Oh, Jesus!

Marcia reaches down, but before she can pick the Robot up, a pair of WHEELS descends from its sides and it whirs across the room and under the couch.

Marcia takes a step forward.

A menacing GROWL comes from beneath the couch.

          MARCIA

            Oh my God.

She pulls her feet up onto her chair and hugs her knees to her chest.

A faint red glow emanates from beneath the couch.

>**MARCIA**
>
>Oh my God.

Another GROWL rises into the air.

Marcia jumps from her chair, runs across the room, grabs her shoes and keys, and bolts out the door.

EXT. STREET/PAYPHONE - NIGHT

Marcia stands in the street, talking on a payphone.

>**MARCIA**
>
>Look, I just think there's something wrong.

INT. CASEWORKER'S OFFICE - NIGHT

[Intercut with Marcia on the street]

The Caseworker sits at her desk.

>**CASEWORKER**
>
>Every child has his bad days.

>**MARCIA**
>
>I'm not talking about a child; I'm talking about this machine. It's defective. Something's gone wrong.

>**CASEWORKER**
>
>Do you want us to pick him up?

Marcia hesitates.

>**CASEWORKER**
>
>If there's a software problem, we'll let you try again. But if there's not...

>**MARCIA**
>
>I just...

CASEWORKER

We can have someone there in an hour.

MARCIA

Wait. Listen.

(plaintive)

I just don't know why it's acting this way.

CASEWORKER

It's just like that sometimes, Marcia. Some children...

(beat)

You know, when my son was two, the cat had kittens. And one day when I was in the other room, David got into their box and just... He killed three of those little kittens. Just squeezed them to death. I couldn't believe it. I just could not... But he's fine, Marcia. He's an English major -- a dorm counselor. A gentle, happy young man.

(beat)

But at that moment... I hated him.

(beat)

Every child looks like a monster sometimes. But those moments pass, Marcia. They really do.

EXT. STREET - NIGHT

Marcia stares into space, still holding the phone to her ear.

INT. LIVING ROOM - NIGHT

Marcia opens the door and steps into the apartment.

The place has been trashed, as if a pack of angry terriers had chewed everything within reach to pieces.

Tamlyn Tomita in "My Robot Baby"

Photo by Wesley Law

> **MARCIA**
>
> Oh, no.

Faint WHINES and WHIRS hit the air.

Marcia spins.

There's nothing in sight.

> **MARCIA**
>
> C'mon, baby.

Very gingerly, Marcia bends down to peer under the couch.

> **MARCIA**
>
> Hello?

A HUM hits the air.

Marcia spins to catch a glimpse of a SHADOW flitting across the room into the kitchen.

INT. KITCHEN - NIGHT

Marcia steps into the kitchen.

The tablecloth has been pulled off of the breakfast table.

Silverware, utensils, and broken dishes are scattered across the floor.

Marcia picks up the broomstick from the corner of the kitchen.

She hangs by the door, holding the broom out in front of her.

> **MARCIA**
>
> Hello...

Nothing.

She bends down slowly to peer under the dining room table.

There's nothing there.

She steps inside the room and works her way around to peer into the corner.

A terrible CLATTER hits the air.

Marcia spins.

Something round and rose-colored rolls toward her.

She SCREAMS and jumps backward, stumbling and falling to the ground, flailing in panic.

The thing on the floor rolls over on its side.

It's a pink rice cooker.

> **MARCIA**
>
> Oh, FUCK me.

INT. LIVING ROOM - NIGHT

The sound of banging pots and pans comes from the kitchen.

> **MARCIA (O.S.)**
>
> Fuck me fuck me FUCK ME!

A WHIMPERING sound hits the air.

The CLATTERING stops.

Marcia steps out of the kitchen. She holds the broom in one hand and a big, heavy saucepan with the other.

Another WHIMPER.

Marcia steps forward.

Silence.

She looks around the room.

Every corner looks like a place where something horrible and sharp could be hiding.

> **MARCIA**
>
> Where are you?
>
> (louder)
>
> Where are you?
>
> (louder)
>
> Where are you, you little fucker!

A SCREAM hits the air.

Marcia quails in terror.

The SCREAM trails off into a thin WAIL, then a broken SOB.

Marcia's face changes.

Her eyes fall on the closet door.

The SOBS continue.

There's a baby CRYING in there.

INT. CLOSET - NIGHT

Marcia pushes opens the closet door.

The Robot lets out a frightened SQUEAK, then sobs uncontrollably, its face pressed against a laundry bag.

Marcia blinks.

Then leans against the side of the doorway.

Slowly she slides down to squat in the doorway of the closet.

INT. YOUNG MARCIA'S CLOSET - NIGHT (MARCIA'S MEMORY)

Marcia's mother squats in the doorway of the closet, staring blankly into space.

The six-year-old Marcia, her face streaked with tears, stares at her mother.

CLOSE ON:

MARCIA'S POV OF:

Mrs. Ito's desolate profile.

Mrs. Ito turns to Marcia.

Her eyes are completely empty.

INT. CLOSET - CONTINUING

The adult Marcia's face wrenches up. She fights it. But it comes, in a great, rending SOB.

The little Robot turns to look at her.

> **MARCIA**
>
> I'm so sorry.

Marcia covers her face and weeps, in big, wracking, sobs of grief.

The Robot stares, its little light pulsing gently. Then it wheels forward and presses its face against Marcia's side.

Marcia pulls her hands away from her face.

The Robot gazes up at her, burbling softly.

Marcia stares down at the Robot. Then wraps her arms around it and weeps.

DISSOLVE TO:

EXT. PARK - DAY

Marcia sits on a bench, talking on her cell phone as CHILDREN play on the jungle gym, swinging from the bars, lining up to sail down the slide.

> MARCIA

(into the phone)

> Look, Doug. When I say today, I mean today. As in today. Okay? Okay.

Familiar MALE LAUGHTER hits the air.

Marcia turns to see Roy walking towards her, laughing as the TODDLER perched on his shoulders drips ice cream onto his head.

Roy looks around the park, not seeing Marcia.

> MARCIA

> Hey, Roy!

He sees her.

His eyes widen.

> AMANDA (O.S.)

> Hey, baby!

AMANDA, a pretty young woman with another TODDLER in tow, walks up to Roy and gives him a kiss on the cheek.

> AMANDA (cont'd)

(laughing)

> Omigod, you've got chocolate all over you! We better get going --
> Rosie's expecting us at five and you gotta get cleaned up...

Roy smiles at Amanda as she steers him off, but looks back at Marcia over his shoulder.

She smiles and raises a hand.

He gives her a little half-smile, then disappears around the trees.

Marcia's smile fades. A kind of pain creases her features.

> CHILD (O.S.)

> Hey, Mom! Look at me!

Marcia turns toward the playground.

A small TOT whoops as he heads down the slide.

> **CHILD (O.S.)**
>
> Ma!

Marcia jerks as a child's big wheel tricycle bumps into her.

> **MARCIA**
>
> Whoa!

She looks down, and there he is, perched in the tricycle, beaming up at her:

About three feet tall, a fat, round little body with spindly little arms and legs --

Her Robot Baby.

> **MARCIA**
>
> Hey, big guy.

> **ROBOT**
>
> Jonah said I could have his duck, but then he didn't have a duck. So I
> said, where's your duck? And he said --

Marcia smiles, her eyes filled with pride and joy.

DISSOLVE TO:

EXT. PARK - DAY

Marcia heads down the path, talking and laughing with the Robot as he pedals alongside her in his tricycle.

FADE TO BLACK.

TITLE CARD: CLAY

FADE IN.

<u>**INT. STUDIO - DAY**</u>

JOHN LEE, a wiry old man, slams a lump of clay onto the table and begins to knead.

He closes his eyes.

His fingers probe into the clay, as if searching for something deep inside.

His brow furrows with concentration. A thin layer of sweat forms on his face.

This is hard work for such an old man.

He opens his eyes.

A faceless, armless, female figure has begun to emerge from the clay.

John wipes his forehead and kneels down for a better look.

There's a hint of emotion in the piece -- the figure's torso is twisted; its head tilted back.

But it's unformed, uncertain.

John straightens up and gazes across the room at the photos on the wall:

Simple, beautiful, abstract sculptures of rounded shapes in public spaces.

He looks back down at the semi-formed lump before him.

No good.

John begins to COUGH.

He tries to suppress it but can't.

He reaches for the figure, but the coughing overtakes him.

He leans against the table, squashing the figure.

<u>**INT. LIVING ROOM/KITCHEN - EVENING**</u>

Tired and dirty, John enters the apartment.

>   **FEMALE VOICE**
>   Hello, John!

John grunts. He walks to the kitchen sink and begins to scrub his hands and arms.

>   **FEMALE VOICE**
>   Trouble with the kiln again?

JOHN

Didn't get that far.

FEMALE VOICE

I'm sorry.

JOHN

I don't wanna talk about it.

FEMALE VOICE

All right.

John pulls a beer from the refrigerator.

FEMALE VOICE

You won't want to hear this, but there's a message from Tommy...

A BEEP sounds, then:

YOUNG MAN'S VOICE

(on edge)

Hey, Dad. This is a business call... Just wondering what's going on. We were expecting a status report today...

John makes a face and steps into the living room.

INT. LIVING ROOM - CONTINUING

A lovely young WOMAN lounges on the couch.

It's HELEN, John's wife.

HELEN

Hey, Johnny.

John's face softens.

JOHN

Helen.

> **HELEN**
>
> So he wants you to call him --

For an instant, HELEN BREAKS APART into a ripple of tiny squares.

> **JOHN**
>
> Dammit.

John taps at a small BLACK BOX sitting on the bookshelf.

Helen breaks up again, then reappears.

> **JOHN**
>
> Gotta get this thing fixed.

> **HELEN**
>
> It's all right.

John sits down on the couch.

> **HELEN**
>
> Are you okay?
>
> He coughs once, takes a breath, swallows hard.

> **JOHN**
>
> I'm fine.

She stands.

> **HELEN**
>
> You're tired. Put on your sleepers and come to bed.

> **JOHN**
> (sharply)
>
> Can you give me half a second?

Helen smiles, gently.

> **HELEN**
>
> All right.

He gazes up at her.

She is lovely.

She turns and walks toward the bedroom door.

Halfway across the room, she shimmers and vanishes.

John takes another swig of his beer, continues sitting for half a second, then cracks a half-smile at himself, stands up, and heads toward the bedroom.

INT. BEDROOM - NIGHT

There's no one in the room but John.

He sits on the bed, pulling on a sleek pair of long johns.

He feels under the collar of the long johns and pulls out a short cable which terminates in a small plug.

He reaches behind his ear.

His eyes fall on the photo on his dresser:

JOHN AND HELEN, both in their thirties, gaze solemnly at the camera in a studio portrait shot.

John's fingers trace a small socket behind his ear.

He closes his eyes, then fits the plug into the socket.

INT. BEDROOM - NIGHT

A much younger John opens his eyes, pushes back the covers, and slides into bed beside Helen.

She smiles sleepily, pulls him close, and kisses him softly.

Tim Kang in "Clay"

> **HELEN**
>
> That's better, isn't it?
>
> **JOHN**
>
> I suppose.

HELEN

You suppose!

She laughs and play-bats him on the back of the head.

He grins and pulls her close.

They make love.

INT. BEDROOM - LATER

The Young John lies on his back. Helen dozes, her head on his chest.

He strokes her hair.

She smiles and opens her eyes.

Eisa Davis and Tim Kang in "Clay"

JOHN

Helen.

HELEN

John.

Her eyes radiate perfect peace.

JOHN

(softly)

I don't know what I'm doing.

HELEN

You're lying in bed in the arms of your loving wife.

JOHN

Yeah.

But that's not it.

HELEN

The sculpture?

JOHN

It's not coming together. It's like it's not <u>in</u> there...

HELEN

You'll find it.

JOHN

You're so sure?

HELEN

Yes.

He gazes at her, probingly.

HELEN

What?

JOHN

I don't deserve you.

She smiles and snuggles into his neck.

INT. BEDROOM - NIGHT

The Old John sleeps peacefully.

He's alone, his arms wrapped around a pillow.

INT. STUDIO - DAY

The Young John works with the clay.

His fingers move with sure, smooth strength.

The clay takes form...

In fragments, we see his hands forming the clay into perfect curves and shapes...

The Young John breathes, free and easy.

A slow smile slips over his face.

COUGHING breaks the air.

On the other side of the room, the Old John presses a handkerchief to his mouth.

As if in a trance, the Young John continues to work, paying no attention to his double.

The Old John suppresses his coughing and moves closer.

The Young John draws his hands back from the sculpture.

The Old John steps closer, eager to catch a glimpse...

But as soon as the sculpture comes into view,

BLINDING WHITE LIGHT surges from the spot, making it impossible to see.

>**OLD JOHN**
>
>Wait!

INT. BEDROOM - MORNING

The Old John jerks awake.

He's alone in bed, light from the window streaming over his face.

>**JOHN**
>
>Goddammit.

>**HELEN'S VOICE**
>
>Are you all right?

>**JOHN**
>
>Yeah, yeah.

>**HELEN'S VOICE**
>
>Tommy called again...

John makes a face and heaves himself out of bed.

INT. BOARDROOM - DAY

John's son TOMMY, a young man in a business suit, stands in the background, watching nervously as:

The Old John gazes down at a diorama of a public square.

There's a tiny, empty pedestal in the middle of the diorama.

A few EXECUTIVES in suits hover around him.

>**EXECUTIVE**
>
>You know we have total confidence in you, John.

>**EXECUTIVE 2**
>
>But the public opening is just six weeks away.

JOHN

I've been having some trouble with the kiln. But I'm nearly done with the --

John begins to cough.

Tommy steps forward and kneels by his father.

TOMMY

All right, Dad. You need some water?

But John can't seem to stop coughing.

The Executives exchange looks.

INT. DOCTOR'S OFFICE - DAY

A hearty young DOCTOR strides into the room.

DOCTOR

You're a lucky man, Mr. Lee!

The Doctor gestures at a monitor. A digital x-ray of John's lungs appears.

DOCTOR

See all those dark blotches? That's the infection.

The blotches run throughout John's lungs.

DOCTOR

Twenty years ago, a little penicillin could have cleared this all up, but these bugs are getting a little too strong for us, now. I'd say this ol' body of yours has maybe a year.

John stares at him blankly.

JOHN

So what's the lucky part?

The Doctor gives him a surprised look.

DOCTOR

Well, this qualifies you for immediate scanning!

JOHN

Scanning.

The doctor pulls a card from his pocket and hands it to John.

DOCTOR

They'll slot you right in. The hospital's already forwarded your files.

The card reads: Forever, Inc.

DOCTOR

Exciting as hell, John. I envy you. You're gonna see everything, you know? Be everywhere, know all there is.

He grins.

DOCTOR

Things are just beginning for you, old man.

INT. STUDIO - LATER

The Old John sits at the table, staring at his clay. A woman's torso has begun to push its way out of the lump.

Helen sits across the table, gazing at the sculpture.

HELEN

You're doing something new.

JOHN

I'm fucking it up.

HELEN

You'll figure it out.

John looks up at Helen. She ripples slightly.

He taps at the black box sitting on the table.

Her image stabilizes.

He eyes her closely, then turns back to his sculpture and begins working at the clay, using her as a model.

HELEN

So that's why you brought me here.

JOHN

You mind?

HELEN

Of course not.

Time passes.

INT. STUDIO - DAY

John stares at his sculpture.

The piece has taken on Helen's features and figure. But there's no emotion, no spirit in the clay.

He stares at Helen sitting across the table. She gazes into space.

JOHN

Where are you?

HELEN

I'm right here.

JOHN

Where else?

Pause.

HELEN

I'm watching the sun set over a sheep farm near Oxford. I'm taking notes at the Senate hearings on the Arizona virus. I'm across town talking with Tommy. I'm having a dream about a red turtle in a big pink envelope... And I'm singing a lullaby to a little girl in a children's hospital in Bogota.

John stares at her.

> **JOHN**
>
> I'm jealous.

She turns to gaze at him.

> **HELEN**
>
> It's hard to understand, isn't it?

> **JOHN**
>
> You don't love me.

> **HELEN**
>
> I do. So very much.

> **JOHN**
>
> You love everybody.

Beat.

> **HELEN**
>
> It'll all make sense soon.

He stares at her.

She gazes into space.

INT. HOSPITAL - NIGHT

A little Latino GIRL with a bandaged hand lies in bed.

Helen's digital image sits in the corner of the room, singing a sweet, soothing LULLABY.

INT. STUDIO - DAY

John looks down into the empty eyes of his sculpture.

An unexpected SOB rips out of him.

> **HELEN**
>
> John...

Fighting his sobs, John reaches for the top of the black box.

HELEN

John, wait...

John presses the switch on the top of the box.

Helen shimmers and disappears.

INT. HOSPITAL - NIGHT

Helen stops singing for an instant.

The little Girl opens her eyes.

Helen begins singing again, as lovely and soothing as before.

The little Girl smiles and closes her eyes.

EXT. CONTRUCTION AREA/PUBLIC SQUARE - DAY

The Old John walks toward a small construction area.

He passes through a gap in the chain link fencing and approaches a wide, low pedestal in the middle of the site.

This is where his sculpture should be.

TOMMY (O.S.)

Hey, Dad.

John looks up to see Tommy stepping though the gap in the fence.

JOHN

What do you want?

TOMMY

I need an excuse to have lunch with my pops?

Smiling, he holds up a couple of bento lunch boxes.

JOHN

(cold)

What do you want?

Tommy and John stare at each other.

Silence.

Tommy pulls a card from his pocket and hands it to his father.

> **TOMMY**
>
> I made an appointment for you.

It's another "Forever, Inc." card.

John stares at his son.

Tommy gives him a small smile.

EXT. PUBLIC SQUARE - CONTINUING

John strides across the square.

Tommy follows close behind.

> **TOMMY**
>
> Dad, come on. You're on the crit list.

> **JOHN**
>
> I don't wanna talk about this.

> **TOMMY**
>
> Well, you're going to have to. You can't even finish the mock-up -- how the hell are you gonna supervise the full-scale?

> **JOHN**
>
> And putting my brain into a computer'll make that possible?

> **TOMMY**
>
> They've worked through that a million ways, Dad. Once you're scanned, you just visualize stuff, ya know? It shows up on screens, in the data-bases. They get instant blueprints and whatnot.

> **JOHN**
>
> That's ridiculous.

> **TOMMY**
>
> It works!

JOHN

Not for me. I have to feel it, have it in my hands. I have to <u>experience</u> it, goddammit!

TOMMY

Come on, Dad. When you're scanned, you're gonna know exactly how to do this thing. You're gonna figure it all out, instantly. You know that.

JOHN

Then it won't mean shit, will it?

TOMMY

What?

He and Tommy stare at each other.

TOMMY

I'm not the artist, here...

JOHN

I'm not talking about <u>art</u>, you idiot.

TOMMY

(continuing)

... but you're not talking reasonably here, Dad. You're not making sense. This is your <u>life</u> we're talking about. You can't just throw that away. It's immoral. And it's illegal.

JOHN

What?

Tommy holds out the "Forever, Inc." card.

TOMMY

You have an appointment, Dad. I think you should keep it.

INT. SUBWAY - EVENING

John sits on the subway.

ARCHIE, a young man in a blue Oxford, sits near him.

Archie's phone rings.

>   **ARCHIE**
> (into the phone)
>> Hello?

Beat.

Archie eyes John, then hands him the phone.

>   **ARCHIE (cont'd)**
>> It's for you.

John raises the phone to his ear.

>   **HELEN**
> (over the phone)
>> John.

>   **JOHN**
>> Yeah.

>   **HELEN**
>> I know you're scared, and angry, maybe. But I'm happy. I can't help it. We're going to be together, Johnny. Truly, completely together.

Beat.

>   **HELEN**
>> Come home.

>   **JOHN**
>> I will.

>   **HELEN**
>> You're on the wrong train.

JOHN

Look, I'm gonna give this guy back his phone...

HELEN

Don't shut me out, John. I'm here for you.

JOHN

I gotta go.

He hands the phone back to Archie.

JOHN

Thanks.

ARCHIE

No problem.

(beat)

It's nice when they call, isn't it?

EXT. TRACKS - NIGHT

The train whirs down the tracks, leaving the city.

EXT. MOTEL - NIGHT

John walks from the check-in window of the run-down motel to the door of his room.

INT. MOTEL ROOM - NIGHT

John sits at the table, peering at a map. With his finger, he traces a road leading into a state park.

His hands tremble.

He pauses, rubbing his knuckles.

The PHONE rings.

John turns.

The phone RINGS again.

John stands.

It RINGS again.

John walks over, kneels, and unplugs the phone from the wall.
The television flickers to life.

> **HELEN (O.S.)**
>
> Hello, John.

John turns.
Helen gazes out at him from the television screen.

> **HELEN**
>
> I'm sorry to bother you like this...

John steps forward and turns off the television set.

> **HELEN'S VOICE**
>
> Please, John. You're scaring me.

John scans the room, looking for the source of the voice.

> **JOHN**
>
> I'm scared, too.

> **HELEN'S VOICE**
>
> Then come home.

He lets out a breath.

> **JOHN**
>
> If you know I'm here, they're already on their way.

Silence.
He sits down on the bed.

> **JOHN**
>
> It's over, isn't it?

> **HELEN'S VOICE**
>
> Nothing's over.

Drained, he lies back on the mattress.

HELEN'S VOICE

It'll all make sense --

JOHN

I know. I'll know everything; I'll be everywhere. I'll be filled with peace, love, and understanding, and you and I will live together in perfect joy forever and ever, amen.

Beat.

HELEN

I love you.

JOHN

Did you love me before?

Beat.

HELEN

Not always.

JOHN

Because I was a selfish bastard.

HELEN

Yes.

JOHN

So why do you love me now?

HELEN

People change.

JOHN

I didn't. I'm as bad a man as I ever was.

John sits up and flicks the television back on.

Helen gazes at him.

JOHN

This is all a lie. You... what you're living and feeling is a lie. I don't deserve you. And I don't want to live forever with a happiness I never earned.

HELEN

Everyone deserves love.

He touches the screen, torn and sad.

HELEN

John...

She gazes at him.

A KNOCK sounds on the door.

John looks up in alarm.

MAN'S VOICE

Mr. Lee?

INT. MOTEL HALLWAY - NIGHT

Two men in dark SUITS stand in the hallway. A TECHNICIAN carrying a small case with the "Forever, Inc" logo stands behind them.

SUIT

(to the door)

You have an appointment, sir.

INT. MOTEL ROOM - NIGHT

The door swings open.

John is nowhere in sight.

Helen, on the video screen, points toward the open window.

The sound of an ENGINE STARTING hits the air.

HELEN

Your car.

The Suits spin and head back out the door.

Helen watches them go.

John steps out of the bathroom.

JOHN

Why?

HELEN

I don't know.

They stare at each other.

EXT. STREET - NIGHT

John walks down the street.

The map dangles from one hand.

He begins to cough.

JOHN

Oh, no.

He suppresses the coughing...

Then breaks down into a paroxysm of hacking.

He lowers himself to his knees, squeezing the map of the state park.

DISSOLVE TO:

EXT. STREAM - DAY

John kneels in the shallow water, his arms underwater.

He smiles and raises his hands.

He's holding a big clump of slick, gray clay.

Sab Shimono in "Clay"

Photo by Wesley Law

EXT. STREAM - LATER

John sits on a wide, flat rock at the water's edge, kneading the clay.

EXT. GLADE - EVENING

John sits at an ancient picnic table in an overgrown glade, working the clay between his hands.

EXT. CAMPFIRE - NIGHT

John sits by a flickering campfire, molding and shaping his sculpture.

His fingers glide along a perfect curve of clay.

EXT. BOWER - MORNING

John slowly traces Helen's cheek with his fingers.

They're lying beneath a bower of green saplings and flowering vines.

She opens her eyes.

Sab Shimono and Eisa Davis in "Clay"

> JOHN
>
> Helen.

> HELEN
>
> John.

Her eyes radiate perfect peace, perfect love.

His eyes turn sad.

> JOHN
>
> I wish this were real.

> HELEN
>
> It is.

> JOHN
>
> No.

HELEN

John.

JOHN

What?

HELEN

Did <u>you</u> love <u>me</u>?

John stares at her.

JOHN

You used to get so angry. I'd come home late; you'd wouldn't even look at me. You'd sit there, reading, so hard and cold. I'd be scared to touch you.

She gazes at him.

JOHN

(finally responding to her questioon)

No.

Her eyes slowly fill with tears.

JOHN

You see?

HELEN

It doesn't matter.

JOHN

It does.

HELEN

I won't let you die.

EXT. STREAM - MORNING

John, filthy and ragged, lies alone on the rock alongside the stream.

The Technician runs forward, presses a circular disk to John's chest, and peers at a small hand-held screen.

> **TECHNICIAN**
>
> Looks like we're just in time!

He unlatches his small silver case and pulls out some equipment.

John opens his eyes.

> **JOHN**
>
> Wait...

He turns to gaze at Helen, who kneels beside him on the rock.

The Technician doesn't seem to notice her.

> **JOHN**
>
> Stop them.

The Technician raises a small, gun-like contraption.

> **JOHN**
> (to Helen)
>
> I wanna be real.

> **HELEN**
>
> You'll die.

> **JOHN**
>
> I know.

Tears fill her eyes.

The Technician presses the machine to the side of John's head.

> **HELEN**
>
> I love you.

> **JOHN**
>
> I love you.

Helen raises a hand.

The Technician flies backward.

Tommy and the Suits step forward.

Helen turns toward them.

They tumble backwards.

John stares at the sky.

> **JOHN**
>
> Oh, God.

His eyes widen.

He gasps for breath.

Tears begin to stream down his face.

He GASPS. He stiffens.

His hand squeezes.

Clay oozes out from between his fingers.

He dies.

BLACKNESS.

SLOW FADE IN.

INT. LIVING ROOM - MORNING

The Young John opens his eyes.

They're full of wonder.

He turns to gaze at Helen, who sits on the couch beside him.

> **HELEN**
>
> Where were you?

John blinks, catching his breath. The wonder slowly drains out of his eyes.

> **JOHN**
>
> Dreaming.

HELEN

What happened?

JOHN

I died.

HELEN

How nice.

Tim Kang and Eisa Davis in "Clay"

She smiles at him, a little sadly.

They gaze into each other's eyes.

For an instant, they both break apart into a ripple of tiny squares.

John turns to look across the room.

The black box sits on the bookshelf, its red light pulsing gently.

FADE TO BLACK.

END.

film festival **AWARDS**

2004   Festival Buenos Aires Rojo Sangre: Best Director (Greg Pak), Best Screenplay (Greg Pak)

2004   Semana Internacional de Cine Fantastico de Malaga: Best Picture,
Best Director (Greg Pak), Best Actress (Wai Ching Ho), Best Picture Audience Award

2004   Annapolis Reel Cinema Film Festival: Best of Fest Audience Award

2004   Boston Sci-Fi Film Festival: Best Independent Sci-Fi Feature, Best New Director,
Best New Film Audience Award, SF Hall of Fame Inductee — Greg Pak

2004   Yubari Fantastic Film Festival: Special Jury Award

2004   Sci Fi London International Film Festival: Best Feature Film

2003   St. Louis International Film Festival: Best Screenplay (Greg Pak), Best Actress (Wai Ching Ho)

2003   Marco Island Film Festival: Most Original Film

2003   San Francisco Korean American Media Arts Festival: Best Film

2003   Michigan Independent Film Festival: Best Feature Film Audience Award

2003   Boston Fantastic Film Festival: Audience Award

2003   Rhode Island International Film Festival: Grand Prize, Best Narrative Feature

2003   DC APA Film Festival: Best Narrative Feature Film-

2003   Florida Film Festival: Special Jury Award for Emotional Truth

2003   Puchon International Fantastic Film Festival: Best Director (Greg Pak),
Best Actress (Wai Ching Ho)

2003   Fantastisk Film Festival, Sweden: Best Feature Film Audience Choice Award

2003   ShockerFest Film Festival: Best Science Fiction Film, Best Science Fiction Director (Greg Pak),
Best Science Fiction Actor (Sab Shimono), Best Science Fiction Actress (Tamlyn Tomita),
Best Score (Rick Knutsen)

2003   Asian American International Film Festival: Emerging Director Award

2003   Asian Film Festival of Dallas: Special Jury Award

2003   Film Fest New Haven: Honorable Mention

2002   Hamptons Film Festival: Best Screenplay Award

2002   Association Internationale Du Film D'Animation East: Excellence in Design Award, For
Daniel M. Kanemoto's opening credits animation

about the **AUTHOR**

Greg Pak is an award-winning writer and director whose first feature film, *Robot Stories*, starring Tamlyn Tomita and Sab Shimono, won 35 awards, screened theatrically across the country, and is now available on DVD from Kino International. Greg's feature screenplay *Rio Chino* won the Pipedream Screenwriting Award at the 2002 IFP Market and a Rockefeller Media Arts Fellowship in

Greg Pak, writer and director of Robot Stories

Photo by Paige Barr

2003. Greg is now writing for Marvel Comics, where his projects include *1602: New World*, *Iron Man: House of M*, and the sold-out *X-Men: Phoenix - Endsong* mini-series.

Greg's many short films, including *Fighting Grandpa, Mouse,* and *Asian Pride Porn*, have won awards and screened in dozens of film festivals around the world. Greg edits FilmHelp.com and AsianAmericanFilm.com. He studied political science at Yale University, history at Oxford University as a Rhodes Scholar, and film production at the NYU graduate film program. He is represented by Kara Baker of the Gersh Agency, New York and Sandra Lucchesi of the Gersh Agency, Los Angeles.

4th Annual   August 4th -12th 2005
Asian Film Festival of Dallas
Visit us at www.affd.org or e-mail us at mailbag@affd.org - For information about submitting films, please visit our website.

LOS ANGELES
KOREAN
INTERNATIONAL
FILM FESTIVAL

North America's Premier Korean International Film Festival

The Los Angeles Korean International Film Festival (LAKIFF) is dedicated to the cinema of Koreans, Korean Americans, and other Korean diaspora. Its purpose is to bring about a greater knowledge and appreciation of the cultural richness, diversity, and artistic talent of Koreans worldwide. In addition, LAKIFF strives to encourage individual creativity, cultural exchange, and global communication.

With a large and diverse selection of films and thousands in attendance each year, LAKIFF is the prime festival for watching new and cutting edge films by and about Koreans. It's also the ideal festival to showcase your film! Visit our web site at **www.lakiff.com** for the entry submission form, the current film screening schedule, and ticket information.

Director Chan Wook Park at a Q&A session following the screening of his film, "Sympathy for Mr. Vengeance" during LAKIFF 2004.

Visit **www.lakiff.com** for more information!